SOUTHERN RAILWAY

MAUNSELL MOGULS & TANK LOCOMOTIVE CLASSES

SOUTHERN RAILWAY

MAUNSELL MOGULS & TANK LOCOMOTIVE CLASSES

DAVID MAIDMENT

PEN & SWORD TRANSPORT

AN IMPRINT OF PEN & SWORD BOOKS LTD.
YORKSHIRE ~ PHILADELPHIA

First published in Great Britain in 2018 by
Pen & Sword Transport
An imprint of Pen & Sword Books Ltd
Yorkshire - Philadelphia

ISBN 978 1 52673 213 2

Typeset in Palatino by Aura Technology and Software Services, India
Printed and bound in India by Replika Pvt. Ltd.

Pen & Sword Books Ltd incorporates the Imprints of Aviation, Atlas, Family History, Fiction, Maritime, Military, Discovery, Politics, History, Archaeology, Select, Wharncliffe Local History, Wharncliffe True Crime, Military Classics, Wharncliffe Transport, Leo Cooper, The Praetorian Press, Remember When, Seaforth Publishing and Frontline Publishing.

For a complete list of Pen & Sword titles please contact:

PEN & SWORD BOOKS LTD
47 Church Street, Barnsley, South Yorkshire, S70 2AS, England
E-mail: enquiries@pen-and-sword.co.uk
Website: www.pen-and-sword.co.uk

Or

PEN AND SWORD BOOKS
1950 Lawrence Rd, Havertown, PA 19083, USA
E-mail: Uspen-and-sword@casematepublishers.com
Website: www.penandswordbooks.com

All David Maidment's royalties from this book will be donated to the Railway Children charity [reg. no. 1058991] [www.railwaychildren.org.uk]

Other books by David Maidment:

Novels (Religious historical fiction)
The Child Madonna, Melrose Books, 2009
The Missing Madonna, PublishNation, 2012
The Madonna and her Sons, PublishNation, 2015

Novels (Railway fiction)
Lives on the Line, Max Books, 2013

Non-fiction (Railways)
The Toss of a Coin, PublishNation, 2014
A Privileged Journey, Pen and Sword, 2015
An Indian Summer of Steam, Pen and Sword, 2015
Great Western Eight-Coupled Heavy Freight Locomotives, Pen and Sword, 2015
Great Western Moguls and Prairies, Pen and Sword, 2016
Southern Urie and Maunsell 2-cylinder 4-6-0s, Pen and Sword, 2016
Great Western Small-Wheeled Double-Framed 4-4-0s, Pen & Sword, 2017
The Development of the German Pacific Locomotive, Pen & Sword, 2017
Great Western Large-Wheeled Double-Framed 4-4-0s, Pen & Sword, 2017
Great Western Counties, 4-4-0s, 4-4-2Ts & 4-6-0s, Pen & Sword, 2018

Non-fiction (Street Children)
The Other Railway Children, PublishNation, 2012
Nobody ever listened to me, PublishNation, 2012

Cover photo:
Rebuilt 'River' 31790, formerly 2-6-4T No.790 of 1917, at Tonbridge shed, 26 July 1959. Colin Boocock

Back cover:
Three-cylinder 'N1' 31876 leaving Tonbridge with a stopping passenger train for Ashford, 17 August 1957. Ken Wightman

'W' 2-6-4 freight tank, 31912, at Hither Green, 9 May 1959. R.C. Riley

32135, built as 'E1' 0-6-0T No.135 *Foligno* in 1879, rebuilt in November 1928 as an 'E1/R' 0-6-2T, at Exmouth Junction, 5 July 1957. R.C. Riley

CONTENTS

PREFACE & ACKNOWLEDGEMENTS

This is the tenth book I have written for my publishers, Pen & Sword, and the eighth in the 'Locomotive Portfolio' series, five covering my knowledge and experience of Great Western locomotives and the German railway pacifics. This is the second of three of my series on Maunsell's designs for the South Eastern & Chatham and Southern Railways. Having in the previous and forthcoming two books covered his main passenger locomotives (apart from the 'Lord Nelsons', a class I am wary to document as my own experience of them as a regular commuter was less than flattering!), I am now turning my attention to the less glamorous but ubiquitous mixed traffic classes, in particular his 'N' and 'U' moguls and their three cylinder developments, the 'N1's and 'U1's.

The 'U' 6ft diameter coupled wheel engines were developed from Maunsell's controversial 'K' 2-6-4 tank engines intended for express passenger use between London and the Kent and Sussex Coasts, which were known as the 'Rivers', and the three-cylinder version, A890 *River Frome,* from which the 'U1s' were derived. As is relatively well known,

the complaints of rough–riding and 'rolling' of these tank engines at speed, culminating in the disastrous derailment of A800 near Sevenoaks in August 1927, caused the SR Board to authorise their rebuilding as mogul tender engines, despite the fact that the Inquiry and tests elsewhere pointed to the state of the track as the most significant cause of the problems. The moguls were the Southern Railway's main freight locomotives on the South Eastern and Central Divisions and remained so until dieselisation arrived in the early 1960s. They also dominated secondary passenger services throughout the Southern Railway and its BR successor. I include, as in some of my past books, some of my personal experiences with these engines, especially during my schooldays near the Redhill-Guildford-Reading line where they were the mainstay power and later, some continuing contact with them during the late 1950s when I was commuting to London University daily from my home in Woking.

I am also including short paragraphs and photographs of the Maunsell moguls built by Woolwich Arsenal after the First World War which were

subsequently bought by the Great Southern Railway of Ireland and converted to 5ft 3in gauge and the Metropolitan Railway who had them rebuilt as 2-6-4Ts but – in the light of the 'River' experience – purely for freight working. As this is a book about Maunsell's tank engines also, I'm including the 'W' 2-6-4Ts which were really a freight version of the 'River' tank and similar in many ways to the Metropolitan engines and the 'Z' 0-8-0T of 1929 built by Maunsell for heavy shunting until the diesel shunter made development of the design unnecessary. Lastly, I cannot ignore, given the title of the book, Maunsell's rebuilding of the LB&SCR 'E' 0-6-0T as class 'E1/R' 0-6-2T for specific work on the Southern Railway's West of England branch duties. I finish with a very brief look at the BR Standard locomotives which took over the duties of the Maunsell engines at the end of steam on the Region, engines which had many of the characteristics of the engines they replaced.

I owe so many thanks, as usual, to all those who have helped me put this book together. The sources of my research are listed in the bibliography, especially the RCTS volumes on the engines of the SE&CR. For those who wish for a more detailed technical survey than I have given here, I recommend those authoritative volumes. I owe much also to the photographers and owners of photographic collections who have allowed me to use their images free of charge or at reduced publication fees as once more I'm donating all the royalties from the book to the Railway Children charity (www.railwaychildren.org.uk) which I founded in 1995, and is now, according to a senior United Nations Officer, the largest charity in the world that works exclusively for street children. I have attempted to trace all copyright holders, but if I have missed anyone please contact me via the publisher.

My grateful thanks therefore to the Manchester Locomotive Society (MLS) and its photo archivist, Paul Shackcloth, MLS member Mike Bentley, Pen & Sword's Transport History Commissioning Editor and friend, John Scott-Morgan, Rodney Lissenden and the access he has given me to the coloured slides of Dick Riley, Ken Wightman and David Clark. And thanks also to the Pen & Sword Transport publishing team, Janet Brookes, editor Carol Trow and all at Barnsley who make the effort both pleasurable and worthwhile.

David Maidment
2018
www.davidmaidment.com

Chapter 1

RICHARD MAUNSELL

Richard Maunsell was born at Raheny, County Dublin, in Ireland on '26 May' 1868. His predecessors were land-owners and were in the legal profession, but from an early age the boy showed his primary interest to be engineering. He was one of a large family and attended a Public School, the Royal School at Armagh, in 1882, before training after pressure from his father for a Law degree at Trinity College, Dublin, in 1886. However, the backbone BA course at the university was followed by all students and he was able to specialise in engineering, and was also to benefit from his solicitor father's contacts with the Board of the Irish Great Southern & Western Railway, becoming simultaneously a pupil of H.A. Ivatt at its Inchicore Works, before moving to England through connections between Ivatt and Aspinall of the Lancashire & Yorkshire Railway.

Maunsell had a number of basic depot appointments in the Blackpool and Fleetwood District after experience on the design side and during this time was courting Edith Pearson, whom he had met during his contacts with the Aspinall family. However, Edith's father prevented their engagement until Maunsell was better able to assure him of his career earning prospects, so Maunsell sought a higher paid post and successfully applied to be Assistant District Locomotive Superintendent of the East India Railway based at Jamalpur. The East India Railway was very extensive, the second largest railway in India. Maunsell gained rapid promotion there, and after a spell at Tundla, on the Allahabad-Delhi route, was transferred back to Jamalpur, then as the Principal District Locomotive Superintendent.

He was appointed at the young age of twenty-eight to the post of Assistant Locomotive Engineer and Works Manager at Inchicore in March 1896, and immediately set about the reorganisation and modernisation of the Works. Between 1897 and 1902 the GS&WR increased its network size by 70 per cent through company takeovers, with Inchicore becoming responsible for the replacement and maintenance of the increased locomotive fleet. Richard Maunsell was appointed Locomotive Superintendent on 30 June 1911.

Maunsell's reign at Inchicore, however, was short-lived, for in 1913 he was approached by the South Eastern & Chatham Railway seeking a replacement for their Locomotive, Carriage and Wagon Engineer, Harry Wainwright, who took early retirement. He was appointed in December 1913 and had the immediate task of reorganising Ashford Works, which could not cope with the workload then placed on it, and the organisation of which had become a mess – Wainwright had been a fine engineer but his management skills, especially in later years, were weak.

Many of Wainwright's team were nearing retirement age and Maunsell soon assembled a new and very competent team, including James Clayton from Derby and George Pearson and Harry Holcroft from Swindon, although the onset of the First World War restricted their immediate influence. Maunsell was strong enough to bring about significant changes – partly to counter the influence of Hugh McColl, a dour Scot and autocrat who had been allowed to exert undue influence, possibly beyond his competence, especially during Wainwright's declining years. Maunsell had a major task ahead in managing the Works and the design and construction programme, and the directors recognised his priorities and somewhat belatedly split off the responsibility for managing locomotive and rolling stock performance in traffic.

Richard Maunsell at Ashford, c1914. (G.M.Rial)

In 1914, the Government created the Railway Executive Committee to take charge of the railways during the wartime period, and Maunsell was appointed as Chief Mechanical Engineer to this body. Some of his work involved the overseeing of maintenance of locomotives in Belgium and Northern France,

working under ROD auspices and at the end of the war he was awarded the CBE for his services. However, he still found the time to design his prototype locomotives for the SE&CR, the 'N' class mogul and the 'River' class 2-6-4 express passenger tank engine. Maunsell had been poised to act as the CME of the proposed nationalised railway after the war, but political views changed and the 'Grouping' proposed by Sir Eric Geddes, then Minister of Transport, came about under the Railways Act of 1921, implemented on 1 January 1923.

With Robert Urie's retirement at age sixty-eight, Maunsell was the natural successor as CME of the new Southern Railway, inheriting a fleet of 2,285 steam engines of 115 different classes, with little standardisation. He was a consummate and skilled manager and administrator, and popular with his team and staff. His influence in new steam engine design was circumscribed by the Southern Board's priority of investment in electrification, restricting money available for the wholesale standardisation of the steam stock as happened on the GWR under Churchward and Collett, and Stanier on the LMS. Maunsell was heavily involved, along with electrical engineers H. Jones and A. Raworth, in the development of rolling stock for the Brighton and Portsmouth electrification, developing the steam-hauled stock

he had designed in the mid-1920s. By the time of his retirement, 3,000 coaches of electric stock existed, a tenfold increase from 1923. During this time, the workshops and Maunsell were under great pressure to meet the electrification deadlines and this was achieved despite the stress this caused.

Increasing ill health caused Richard Maunsell to take retirement in 1937, when he was sixty-nine years old. He formally handed over responsibility for the SR Motive Power Department to Oliver Bulleid on 31 October, having had a strong and successful relationship for many years with the Southern's General Manager, Sir Herbert Walker. He left the railway with 1,852 steam engines of 77 classes and a substantially electrified network, retiring to spend his days involved in the life of his local Parish Church, which he and Edith attended regularly in Ashford. He was made an honorary member of the Institute of Mechanical Engineers in 1938 and was often called upon to take organised groups around Ashford Works. His last public appearance was on 7 February 1944 at the Dover Harbour centenary celebrations. He died in March, leaving his wife and married daughter, his only child, and is buried in Bybrook Cemetery, Ashford, a few hundred yards from his house, Northbrooke, where he had lived for thirty-two years.

Chapter 2
THE 'N' & 'N1' 2-6-0S

Design & Construction of the 'N's

Wainwright was confronted with a problem on both passenger and freight fronts. Traffic levels on both were increasing at the end of the century's first decade. Efficient but low powered 0-6-0s (the 'C' class) were inadequate for the freights from Kent coalfields and to the channel ports and the 'D' and 'E' 4-4-0s were struggling with the increased loads, especially the continental boat train traffic, and double-heading was frequently resorted to. Wainwright drew up plans for a 4-6-0 passenger engine and an 0-8-0 goods locomotive, but the Civil Engineer turned both down as incompatible with allowed axleloads over the SE&CR's infrastructure. Problems at the company's works and relationships with the company's Board led to Wainwright taking early retirement and Richard Maunsell inherited the problems to be solved. He modified the ordered 'L' 4-4-0s as a stop-gap while bringing in a new management team and preparing plans for both a passenger and freight engine from very different traditions.

By 1915, despite the other wartime activities for which he was responsible, he had drawn up plans, ably assisted by Derby trained James Clayton and colleagues drawn from Swindon. He presented to the SE&CR Board proposals for a freight 2-6-0 and passenger 2-6-4T sharing many technical features, especially the boiler and valve gear arrangements, both leaning heavily on the learning from Churchward at Swindon. He was given approval to build ten of the moguls and six of the passenger tank engines, but war priorities at the works meant that neither were built until 1917 and then only one prototype version of each. The passenger engine, the 'K' tank, is described later in the next chapter. The mogul, numbered 810, was constructed at Ashford and emerged steamed for the first time at the end of July. After a month of tests in which teething problems were sorted out, the 'N', as it was classified, entered revenue earning service.

Its basic dimensions included two cylinders, 19in x 28in, coupled wheels of 5ft 6in diameter, boiler pressure of 200lbs psi, 1,728½sqft of heating surface, 25sqft grate area, with a permitted axle-load of 17½ tons and total engine and tender weight of 98 tons 13cwt. Water capacity was 3,500 gallons and 5 tons of coal in a tender that bore Clayton's Midland Railway influence. Key features influenced by the latest GWR practice were the taper boiler with higher pressure than the SE&CR had previously used, Belpaire firebox, and the long travel valves of 6⅞in and lap of 1½in, although Walschaerts rather than the GW Stephenson valve gear was selected. Important for Maunsell was the accessibility to key parts of the motion for maintenance purposes, and Maunsell designed his own variant of superheater.

810 soon demonstrated its superiority over the company's previous goods engines and a further fifteen were ordered in November 1917 at a cost of £5,875 each. However, wartime restrictions and priorities still applied and it was not until March 1920 that the first of the production run was ready – 811 – and the end of 1923, after a year of the new Southern Railway, that the last of the fifteen, 825, was delivered. As most were built under the SE&CR order, they were painted in the SE&CR wartime grey livery, except for the last one which appeared in the new SR lined green livery as A825. The earlier engines were repainted as they entered the works for their first

A works photograph of the prototype 'N' 2-6-0 built at Ashford for the SE&CR in 1917.
(Loco Publishing Co./ MLS Collection)

major overhauls between 1924 and early 1926.

A number of experiments were carried out on these engines. From 818 onwards, steam sanding became standard. Lubrication changes were made and from 816 increased brake power was provided. The superheater area was increased. The riding of the engine was fine at freight train routine speeds, but was considered rough when working passenger trains, so some rebalancing took place from 818 onwards, although this did not completely cure the problem. Swindon Works had more refined equipment for this and the wheels of 819 were adjusted there in 1922. Tests were carried out with 812 and 819 up to 75mph, and

while both were satisfactory when ex-works, 812 became rough once it had achieved 20,000 miles after overhaul.

After the war, the best coal supply was restricted to passenger engines and the steaming performance of the 'N's suffered badly. Various local efforts were made to improve the steaming unsuccessfully until a Bricklayers Arms foreman and fitter revised the blastpipe/chimney alignment and various other modifications to 812 which was the worst culprit. Once advised of the unofficial, but successful action, Maunsell called 812 in for trials and discovered that the blastpipe chimney alignment was key. He also had some learned experience from the

GWR 43XX mogul blastpipe which he investigated. Incorporating a temporary stovepipe chimney, it was tested on Paddock Wood-Hither Green 65-wagon freights in comparison with 816 and 818. 817 was then equipped with blastpipe arrangements learned from the tests. 818 performed so badly that Maunsell had the blastpipe arrangements of 817 and 818 exchanged, suspecting accuracy of the trial measurements, and found 818 then performed even worse. Trials with different blastpipe arrangements on 816, 817 and 818 gave coal burned per mile results ranging from 69¾lb (817) to 82½lb (818). Subsequently, 818 was found to have faulty piston rings and was leaking steam. Finally, after

The fourth production 'N' built at Ashford in 1920, on arrival at Bricklayers Arms and posed with shed staff, November 1920.
(Loco Publishing Co./ MLS Collection)

Ashford built 820 posing with traincrew at Bricklayers Arms, 1922.
(MLS Collection)

successful experiments with the Swindon 43XX blastpipe on the new three-cylinder 'N1' 822, a chimney, liner and blower ring based on the Swindon design was applied to all the SR 2-6-0 classes.

Maunsell had been Chairman of the government Association of Railway Locomotive Engineers (ARLE) drawing up possible standard designs when the government of the day was leaning towards post-war nationalisation of the railways, and in this capacity had attempted to get the various company engineers to jointly develop 2-6-0 and 2-8-0 standard classes. This met some reluctance and when the war was over and the engineers returned to their own railways, the development of the standard designs stalled. In 1919, the government was

informed that no new standard designs were available, coinciding with cessation of armaments manufacture and return of soldiers from the continent seeking peacetime jobs. Unemployment and fear of unrest (it was the period of the Russian Bolshevik revolution) led the government to order fifty 2-6-0 and fifty 2-8-0 locomotives from the Woolwich Arsenal armaments factory. As no blueprints for standard locomotives had been completed, the Ministry of Munitions ordered fifty 'N's and fifty Great Central RODs. However, a large number of RODs had already been built and more were now returning from the continent, so the order was changed to 'N's in entirety. Ashford provided drawings to Woolwich Arsenal, but the specialist building of the

boilers was contracted out, with 85 being built by the North British Locomotive Company and 20 by Robert Stephenson & Co.

Major problems and delays occurred due to the lack of experience of railway work at the Arsenal, costs escalated and eventually the government had 100 locomotives on its hands that no-one wanted at the price the government was seeking (£14,000 compared with Ashford's, Eastleigh's and Brighton's estimates of £8-9,000 for building to the same design). The Great Eastern had wanted twenty but, when advised of the cost and delays, withdrew. The SE&CR had been prepared to purchase fifteen, but also declined at that price and a more than ten month delivery time. The government advertised the engines

A826, the first of the Woolwich Arsenal constructed 'N's built in June 1924, seen here in 1926. (Real Photographs/ MLS Collection)

then at bargain prices and all went between March 1923 and November 1925, some going to Ireland and others to the Metropolitan Railway (to be described later). Finally, the Southern Railway contracted to take twenty in 1924 at a cost of £79,000, and were delivered (with some difficulty) to Ashford to finalise, number and paint and A826-A845 entered traffic between June and September 1924. Another twenty at the same price were ordered in October 1924 and a

final ten in November at £39,500. They were mainly engine parts and they were assembled at Ashford and fitted with spare SR boilers. These thirty engines left Ashford Works over the first nine months of 1925, numbered A846-A875. A866 was displayed at the Wembley Exhibition. The Southern Railway then purchased remaining unused parts from Woolwich Arsenal consisting of 11 boilers, 37 cylinder castings, 5 sets of main frames, 38 pairs of coupled wheels, 17 Bissel

trucks, 7 sets of tender parts and wheels, 31 chimneys and pipes, brake shoes, coupling rods and other miscellaneous fittings, all for the princely sum of £11,950! Much of this was then used in the rebuilding of the 'K River' tanks, the construction of the 1929 'U' class (A610 – A629) and five 3-cylinder 'N1's. The total loss to the British taxpayer from this ill-founded government initiative has been calculated as in excess of £1 million – a huge sum in 1920.

Woolwich Arsenal constructed A866, exhibited at the Wembley Exhibition, 1925. (LCGB/K. Nunn/John Scott-Morgan Collection)

Brand new A868, constructed at Ashford from Woolwich Arsenal parts, on a freight at Canterbury, July 1925. A poster in the background is publicising a newspaper article about the 1922 Horatio Bottomley political/financial scandal. (W.J. Reynolds/John Scott-Morgan Collection)

A variety of faults was found with the new engines sent by the Southern Railway management to replace Drummond locomotives west of Exeter – piston valve trouble, poor steaming, loose tyres and hot boxes, mainly due to faulty workmanship. The Woolwich engines were only achieving 30-35,000 miles between general repairs compared with 65-70,000 for the Ashford built engines and works inspections even found some of the tender frames out of alignment. Six 3,500 gallon Maunsell tenders were found and eventually, despite crew scepticism, the Woolwich engines in the West of England gave excellent service.

Once these engines had established a good reputation, a final order for fifteen further engines of the class was placed in 1930 and Ashford built Nos.1400-1414 between July 1932 and January 1934. They differed from the earlier engines having a stronger frame, front footsteps, 'U1' pattern chimney, modified blast pipe and 4,000 gallon tenders with turned-in top. 1407-1414 exchanged tenders with 'U' 1610-1617 as the tenders were fitted for right hand drive, whereas those specific locomotives had been built for left hand drive operation (for the South Western ex-LSWR section). The weight was increased to 103 tons 12 cwt and axleload to 18 tons.

A number of experiments were carried out on the class over the years – A819 was fitted with a Worthington feed water heater and pump in 1924. A816 had a much more extensive experiment, with a steam conservation system, devised by a Scottish marine engineer, being fitted and tested in 1930. Despite electrification, steam power was going to be needed for freight traffic for many years. Steam from the cylinders passed into a cooler and then into a compressor before re-entering the boiler and reused. Trials commenced in August 1931, modifications were made and the engine was retested in December 1931. After more modifications, tests in April 1932 were encouraging, until a complete failure occurred. Tests resumed in the summer of 1932 and further modifications were made in 1933. Troubles were by now restricted to the draughting fans, but with pressures from the Depression and electrification taking priority, A816 was stored and the equipment was removed in 1935. In 1931, a newly patented valve gear was accepted for trial and 1850 was fitted with modified cylinders and valve gear and tested in comparison with 1413. Improved economy up to 50mph was noted, but knocking was heard at higher speeds and the valve gear suddenly disintegrated when passing Woking at speed in March 1934. By this time the inventor had died and the experiment was not pursued.

One further development which was not really an experiment, but became a standard for all Southern larger engines, was the provision of smoke deflectors in the 1930s after a series of tests with different forms on 'King Arthurs' at the end of the 1920s. One other important development was the provision of new frames to twelve 'N's between 1931 and 1938 – not modified, but straight replacements as some of the older engines were needing

1932 Ashford built 1405 with smoke deflectors and 4,000 gallon tender, c1935. (MLS Collection)

A819, fitted with Worthington feed water pump at Bricklayers Arms, c1925. (Real Photographs/John Scott-Morgan)

1850 at Eastleigh Works after fitting with the patented new valve gear by A.T. Marshall of Harrogate, fitted with indicator shelters for staff use during road testing, c1933. (John Scott-Morgan Collection)

Two photographs of A816 during the experiments with steam heat conservation carried out between 1931 and 1933, seen here after final modifications at Eastleigh Works in June 1933. (MLS Collection)

major frame repairs (1810-1815, 1820, 1823 and 1832 and 1847 of the Woolwich engines). Before the Grouping, mileage between main repairs was only around 60,000 but this was gradually increased to 80,000 as the aim for all SR 2-6-0s. Pre-war, the highest mileages between repairs were run by the 1932 14xx series, as might be expected, with a couple (1406 and 1407) exceeding 100,000.

Despite the changes to the Southern Railway livery instituted by Bulleid in 1938, the 2-6-0s

continued to be painted in the Maunsell livery of lined sage green with numerals on the tender. The lining was omitted from September 1939 as a war economy until January 1940 when Bulleid style lettering and cabside numerals were applied, then from March 1941 the livery was plain black. Malachite green became their livery from September 1946.

In 1947, the Southern Railway included some of the 'N' class for the government inspired oil-burning project to relieve the

pressure on coal supplies and 1831 was converted and allocated to Fratton where oil facilities existed. It worked trial freight and passenger services from there successfully, but the scheme foundered in 1948 because of shortage of foreign currency to pay for the oil and 1831 was converted back to coal firing in November, having run just over 30,000 miles as an oil-burner.

At nationalisation, all eighty engines entered British Railways stock and were numbered 31400-

1922 built 1817 at Hither Green, still in Maunsell Southern Railway livery, 3 June 1939. (MLS Collection)

31414 and 31810-31875 (excluding the 'N1' 31822). Until the new BR number scheme was approved, former SR engines received a small 's' before their numbers to distinguish them from other Region's engines with similar numbers (e.g. the 'N's shared numbers with the LNER 'K3' 2-6-0s). The following 'N's received the 's' prefix: 1405, 1813, 1814, 1825, 1832, 1838, 1858, 1871. All the 'N's were now being painted plain black until October 1948, when the BR mixed traffic lined black was approved for application to all the Southern Region moguls.

The Southern moguls ran comparable mileages between general repairs as similar classes on other Regions, although not as high as the new BR standard classes which had been designed with ease of maintenance in mind. Maintenance of the 'N's was relatively easy compared with older SR classes as most parts were accessible, but in the 1950s, the frames of the moguls gave concern. At the design stage, the weight of the engines was important because of the limits imposed by the civil engineer and the thickness of the frames was kept to the minimum with the result that this became a

major weakness, especially with the two-cylinder moguls. Cracks and frame distortions occurred and this was becoming a major problem by 1953. Electrification programmes were in hand, but steam would be required for freight work as it was unsafe to electrify goods yards and sidings with the third rail system, so reframing of the most badly affected moguls became policy in 1954. Initially, the whole frame was renewed, but subsequently it was decided that renewing just the front end of the frame would suffice. The reframed engines also received new cylinders and outside steam pipes.

1831 converted to oil-burning at Eastleigh in 1947. (John Scott-Morgan Collection)

s1825 at Brighton, renumbered with the initial 's' after nationalisation, 1948. (MLS Collection)

s1814 with the initial Southern Region numbering and lettering after nationalisation, 1949. (MLS Collection)

31846 in Southern Railway wartime black livery but renumbered post-nationalisation, at Stewarts Lane, 25 May 1948. (MLS Collection)

1922 Ashford built 31821 after repainting in the BR mixed traffic lined black livery, 6 September 1952. (MLS Collection)

31852 under general repair at Eastleigh Works, c1958. (MLS Collection)

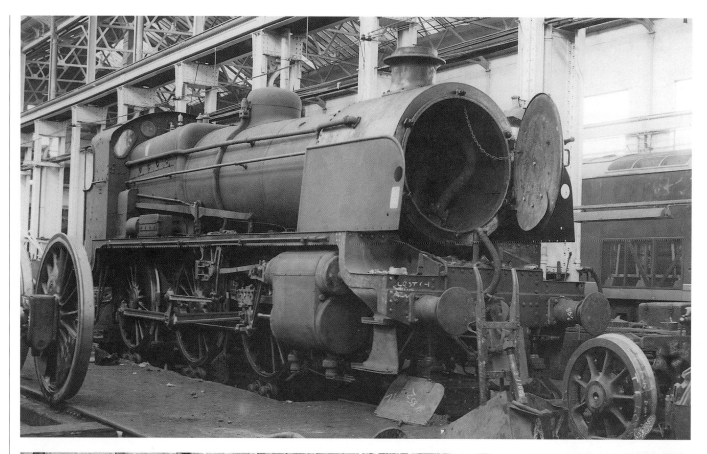

The second 'N', built in 1920, stands at Stewarts Lane shed, 30 March 1959. (R.C. Riley)

31811 again undergoing heavy overhaul at Eastleigh Works alongside rebuilt 'Battle of Britain' 34056 *Croydon*, 6 April 1963. (Roy Hobbs/Online Transport Archive)

The following 'N's received full frame renewal between 1955 and 1961 (exact dates of renewal are in the appendix): 31406, 31413, 31829, 31833, 31835, 31837, 31845, 31848, 31855, 31858, 31863 and 31871. The following engines received new front ends: 31400, 31405, 31408, 31830, 31831, 31838, 31840, 31842, 31843, 31846, 31853, 31854, 31862, 31864, 31868, 31869, 31874. 31848 ran for a time without smoke deflectors (October 1955-February 1957) as it was thought the new BR blast pipe and chimney arrangements would obviate the need, but experience proved this false. Various other detail changes were made during the frame rebuilding affecting AWS provision, live steam injectors, spark arresters, feed water treatment and manganese liners to the coupled wheel axleboxes. The changes were successful and not only reduced maintenance costs but also improved steaming (the new blastpipe arrangements) and crews found them improved in performance.

By 1960 diesels suitable for freight work on the Southern appeared (the class '33' D6500 series) and reframing intended for a further eleven 'N's was cancelled and major repairs ceased for the class in June 1962. Engines requiring heavy frame repairs were withdrawn, although Eastleigh, after the closure of Ashford Works in 1962, did get approval to repair six

31830 showing very clearly the revised shape of its renewed front end, Eastleigh, 11 August 1962. (Colin Boocock)

'N's in 1963 despite only two of these being reframed engines. The first two withdrawals were surprisingly from the later 314xx series, 31409 and 31414 both having serious firebox damage and were condemned with only around 700,000 miles run. The July 1963 adoption of the lines west of Salisbury by the Western Region and its pressure to reduce steam operations, especially in its Plymouth Division, saw the Exmouth Junction 'N's threatened. They received some additional 'N's at the expense of 'S15s' repatriated, but five West Country

moguls were withdrawn that year and only five remained active there when all the West Country services were dieselised in September 1964.

Southern Region withdrawals were also heavy in 1964 and by the end of the year only twelve remained in traffic – 31405 and 31411 , 31816, 31831, 31862, 31866 and 31873 at Redhill and 31401, 31408, 31811, 31842 and 31858 at Guildford. The Tonbridge-Reading DMU service commenced in January 1965, leaving just a few mainly ECS and van workings, and the final survivors into 1966

were three of the 1932 Ashford built batch, 31405, 31408 and 31411. The last two, 31405 and 31408, were withdrawn in June 1966. One of the highest mileages seems to have been reached by the 1917 prototype, 31810, condemned in March 1964, having run 1,066,244 miles. The highest recorded of all was a comparative latecomer, an engine made of Woolwich parts assembled at Ashford in the summer of 1925, 31870, with 1,110,161 miles to its credit. It was withdrawn in April 1964. One would expect the last survivors to have run up the highest mileages, but the very last

31857, an Exmouth Junction 'N', at Padstow a year before its transfer to the Western Region Plymouth Division, 8 August 1962.
(MLS Collection)

1932 built 'N' 31408, destined to be one of the last class survivors, stands ready for duty in Wimbledon Yard, 2 December 1962. It was one of the 'N's that received frame front-end renewal (in April 1957).
(R.C. Riley)

31860, at Exmouth Junction shortly before its November 1963 withdrawal by the Western Region, 17 August 1963. (MLS Collection)

31830, an Exmouth Junction engine for many years, at Brighton where it was allocated in late 1962 as one of several 'N's to replace the ex-LB&SCR 'K' 2-6-0s, most of which were withdrawn at the end of the year, 5 October 1963. (MLS Collection)

31870, which ran 1,110,161 miles in its 38½ year life, at Redhill shed, equipped with a 4,000 gallon turned-top tender, 5 October 1963. (MLS Collection)

31814, one of the first Ashford built production run 'N's, in its final year of 'grime' at Redhill , 11 April 1964. It was withdrawn three months later. (David Clark)

31411 and 'Rebuilt River' 31803 at Eastbourne during the LCGB *Wealden* railtour, 13 June 1965. (Roy Hobbs/Online Transport Archive)

31866 at Brighton at the end of its stint on the Steyning 'farewell' railtour, 5 December 1965. (Roy Hobbs/Online Transport Archive)

were all 1932 built engines and, in any case, diagrams still operated by the 'N's in the last year or so involved low daily mileage.

Thirty-three of the 'N's were broken up at Eastleigh with nearly all the rest going to private scrap dealers in Morriston, Newport, Barry and Risca, all in South Wales. Only 31874 went to Woodham Brothers in Barry, which piece of fortune enabled just the one 'N' class mogul to be preserved.

Operation of the 'N's

810 started regular work in mid-August 1917 with an overnight freight from Bricklayers Arms Yard to Ramsgate, a morning freight train to Richborough, and then on to Chislehurst and light engine back to Bricklayers Arms shed. Weekend turns involved Hither Green-Tonbridge goods work.

The 'N' was allowed 65 wagons between London and Tonbridge and 85 thereafter to Dover. 810 had good route availability over the former SER lines excluding branches, but it was not so easy on the ex LC&DR lines, with many restrictions.

810 during initial testing was able to exert 1,000 horsepower when operated at its optimum output, 50 mph, 25 per cent cut-off, full regulator. There were further trials from January 1922 with the first production run locomotives built in 1921/2. 813 was tested with a 650 ton freight between Hither Green and Ashford whilst 818 was set a 950 ton freight over the 21.4 miles from Paddock Wood to Ashford, which it covered in 61 minutes. With full regulator and cut-off adjusted for gradient, 818 maintained 30mph on the virtual

level track, though it suffered bouts of indifferent steaming.

Once tests were over and routine work commenced the settled allocation in 1925 of the first fifteen 'N's was:

Ashford:	A812, A818
Battersea:	A815, A816, A820, A823
Dover:	A819
Bricklayers Arms:	A810, A811, A813, A814, A817, A821, A824, A825

There had been some trial running from Tonbridge and Redhill depots, particularly over the heavily graded route to Reading. A816 and A825 were tried on the Western Section working from Guildford and Basingstoke to Bournemouth, Salisbury and Exmouth Junction.

820 on a 'race special' consisting entirely of SER crimson lake Pullman cars, in the Chipstead Valley en route to Tattenham Corner, Epsom, c1923. (John Scott-Morgan Collection)

A826-A845 were delivered between June and September 1924 purchased direct from Woolwich Arsenal and A846-A865 were ordered in October 1924. Assembly commenced in January 1925, and the last ten Woolwich engines, A866-A875, were completed by September that year. A826-A860 were allocated to the Southern's Western Section following the successful trials of A816 and A825 as follows:

Salisbury:	A834, A845, A851
Barnstaple:	A839, A841, A849, A857

Exmouth Junction:	A826-A833, A835-A838, A840, A842-A844, A846-A848, A850, A852 – A856, A858-A860

Despite the successful trials with the Ashford built locomotives, the Woolwich engines were not well received in the West Country where they suffered poor steaming, loose tyres, piston valve trouble and hot boxes. Much of the problem was due to defective assembly or poor workmanship at Woolwich as the staff there were unaccustomed to building railway locomotives and the first general overhaul was planned for just 30-35,000 miles, half that of the Ashford engines, when many of the defects were corrected. After that the Woolwich engines performed as well as the Ashford ones.

The last fifteen engines remained on the Eastern Section, allocations being:

Battersea:	A862, A863, A866-A870, A875
Redhill:	A861, A864
Bricklayers Arms:	A865, A871-A874

They also gave greater trouble than the Ashford fifteen, but the

A860 on trial in the West Country seen here at Barnstaple alongside Adams 'Jubilee' 0-4-2 No.628, 21 July 1925. (H.C. Casserley/John Scott-Morgan Collection)

Battersea and Bricklayers Arms fitters had gained experience and matters quickly improved.

Later A851 was tested on passenger services between Salisbury and Yeovil Junction, with 204 tons surmounting Semley summit at 45mph and achieving a maximum speed of 70mph through Gillingham. A837 was tested between Barnstaple and Ilfracombe to assess timings over the 1 in 40 climb from Braunton and the 1 in 36 from Ilfracombe to the summit at Mortehoe. It ran four trials, two in each direction, with 204 tons tare. On the first run from Braunton, which was passed at 50mph, it took no less than 23 minutes to reach the summit 5¾ miles away, nearly stalling. It did better on the second run, taking 21¾ minutes from a standing start at Braunton, minimum speed at the summit, 12mph. From Ilfracombe the 'N' was worked almost flat out over the 3¼ miles, taking 16¾ minutes on the first run, and 14¾ on the second when cut-off was advanced half way up the bank from 60 to 66 per cent! Maximum load for service trains was fixed at 180 tons. However, once the 'U' moguls had been introduced, appropriate passenger work, apart from in Devon and Cornwall, was rarely undertaken by the 'N's until the 1950s.

Brand new A852 on a Nine Elms-Southampton Docks freight train between Woking and Brookwood, 1925. (Railway Photographs/MLS Collection)

1832 at Cowley Bridge Junction, Exeter, with a train from Ilfracombe, c1932. (John Scott-Morgan Collection)

The final batch of fifteen locomotives, 1400-1414, built between 1932 and 1934, was spread over the Southern system:

Ashford:	1400 – 1405
Exmouth Junction:	1406 – 1409
Bricklayers Arms:	1410 – 1412
Salisbury:	1413, 1414

1411-1413 were loaned to Redhill in 1934 to work spoil from excavations at Tonbridge required for the construction of the Southern Railway's new dock at Southampton. The Exmouth Junction new engines were allocated to regular work on the heavily graded Ilfracombe line where they were popular with the crews.

The first 'N's allocated to the Central Section were 1810 and 1812 which were transferred to New Cross Gate in 1932 for freight traffic on weekdays and summer excursion traffic at the weekend. These were followed by 1813-1815 which replaced the 'N1's at Eastbourne in 1935 and remained there until the priorities of the Second World War required them elsewhere. 1861 and 1863 were transferred to Norwood Junction in January 1936 and were swapped for 1816, 1869 and 1870 in October 1937.

The 'N's for a short while were put to work on the Oxted services and S.A.W. Harvey, who recorded a prolific number of logs from 1930 to the early 1950s, captured the one below between East Croydon and Eridge.

East Croydon-Eridge
1851
8 chs, 243/260 tons

Miles	Location	Times mins secs	Speed mph	Punctuality
0.0	East Croydon	00.00		T
0.9	South Croydon	02.27		½ L
1.9	Sanderstead	04.09	(1:83 R)	¼ L
3.1	Riddlesdown	06.10	38	
5.0	Upper Warlingham	09.35	sigs	
6.8	Woldingham	13.35	25 (1:100 R)	
9.1	Lime Siding	15.40	60	
9.9	Oxted	18.09		2¼ L
0.0		00.00		
1.1	Hurst Green Jcn	02.18	38	2½ L
3.1	Monks Lane	04.22	67	
5.3	Edenbridge	06.46		¼ L
0.0		00.00		
1.8	Hever	03.22	36	
3.7	Cowden	06.05	52	
6.5	Ashurst	08.45	66	
8.1	Ashurst Junction	10.27		¼ E
9.1	Birchden Junction	11.25		¼ E
10.1	Eridge	12.43		1 E

Mr Harvey commented that the mogul was worked very hard to achieve these times.

Maintenance of the moguls improved during the 1930s and mileages between heavy repairs rose from an average of 60,000 steadily to 80,000 by the onset of the Second World War. The performance of the 1400 series was particularly noteworthy on this score, a couple (Exmouth Junction's 1406 and 1407) exceeding 100,000.

The volume of freight traffic over the Southern Railway routes rose considerably during the war and the Eastbourne engines were sent to Norwood Junction. The Eastern Section engines were at risk from enemy action, but were well used on wartime supplies to the Kent Coast. From around

1942 maintenance deteriorated and Eastern Section freight requirements continued to increase, so in April 1943, a dozen of the West Country engines (1830,1837, 1839, 1840, 1843, 1844, 1846, 1848, 1849, 1852, 1858 and 1859) were reallocated to Bricklayers Arms, replaced by 'T9' 4-4-0s, as holiday traffic in Devon had petered out. Mileages between repairs continued – of necessity – to rise, the record being held by 1411 which ran 135,323 miles between heavy repairs in March 1939 and August 1944. In March 1944 the Southern Railway began to receive WD 2-8-0s which took over the heaviest freight work and eighteen 'N's were repatriated to the West Country and the South Western sheds as follows:

Exmouth Junction:	1821, 1823-1825, 1839, 1843, 1844, 1869-1871
Salisbury:	1872, 1873
Eastleigh:	1865, 1866, 1875
Guildford:	1867, 1868, 1874

Redhill also received a couple (1863 and 1864) and Battersea got 1410-1414. The influx of the 2-8-0s allowed the storage of some very high mileage 'N's and the build-up of repairs was addressed, so that there were enough in reasonable condition when the 'WD's were required on the continent after D-Day. During the immediate preparation for the D-Day landings all the 'N's, and other moguls and freight engines, were pressed into service. After the sudden departure of the 'WD's at the end of 1944, the stored and repaired 'N's were required back in service and transfers and reinstatements took place as follows:

Bricklayers Arms:	1410 – 1414, 1823, 1858, 1859, 1862, 1875
Battersea:	1813, 1824 – 1826
Hither Green:	1817 – 1821
Norwood:	1844, 1852
Salisbury:	1846, 1848
Redhill:	1849
Eastleigh:	1867, 1870, 1874

At the end of the war and the reduction in freight supplies required for the conflict, further reallocations took place and the January 1946 allocation was:

Bricklayers Arms:	1410 – 1414, 1817 – 1821, 1823, 1843, 1850, 1858, 1859, 1862, 1875
Battersea:	1810 – 1813, 1824 – 1826
Ashford:	1400 – 1405
Redhill:	1814 – 1816, 1849, 1863, 1864
Reading:	1857, 1860, 1861
Exmouth Junction:	1406 – 1409, 1828, 1830-1838, 1840 – 1842, 1845, 1847, 1851, 1853 – 1856, 1869, 1871
Eastleigh:	1827, 1829, 1865, 1867, 1870, 1874
Guildford:	1868
Salisbury:	1839, 1846, 1848, 1872, 1873
Norwood:	1844, 1852

The 'N's and 'U's monopolised workings on the Redhill-Reading line ('The Rattler') during the 1950s, right up to their demise at the end of 1964. A number of photographers lived in the area and there is a fine selection of both monochrome and colour slide photos of the moguls taken at work in the area, and I have chosen a number to illustrate their activity over this heavily graded secondary route that was an important thoroughfare to the Western Region and Midlands in both the Second World War and the summer holiday seasons.

31847 waits to depart from Padstow at 1pm with the portion of a train for Waterloo, 27 May 1950. (J.H. Aston/ John Scott-Morgan Collection)

31413 on a Ramsgate-Victoria relief express, passing Newington, 13 June 1953. (R.C. Riley)

31836 on Exmouth Junction shed alongside LMS prototype diesel electric 10000 which has worked the down *Atlantic Coast Express,* 29 May 1953. (C.H.S. Owen/MLS Collection)

31845 at Exeter St David's with the North Devon portion of a Waterloo express, 10 May 1956. (G.D. Whitworth/MLS Collection)

31845 at Meldon with the Plymouth portion of the *Atlantic Coast Express*, 4 June 1959. (J.H. Aston/John Scott-Morgan Collection)

Two photos of 31810 after running through the sand drag at Shortlands Junction with a van train, 11 April 1958. (Ken Wightman)

31411 climbing Sole
Street bank with a
Ramsgate-Victoria relief
train, August 1958.
(Ken Wightman)

31407 with a down van
train leaving Sevenoaks
Tunnel, 21 August 1960.
(David Clark)

31406 between Knockholt and Polhill Tunnel with a Sunday van train from Bricklayers Arms, 4 September 1960. (David Clark)

31871 at St Mary Cray with a Hither Green-Ashford freight train, 6 March 1959. (Ken Wightman)

An 'N' in the West Country – 31831 at Cowley Bridge Junction, Exeter, awaiting the road with a train for the Southern route to Okehampton and Plymouth, 5 July 1961.
(R.C. Riley)

31831 at Cowley Bridge Junction with a train of 'A' Containers on flat wagons for Exmouth Junction Yard, 22 May 1961. 31831 has also had frame renewal.
(MLS Collection)

31831 on a freight at Wadebridge, 20 May 1960. (MLS Collection)

31841 at Okehampton with the Plymouth portion of a Waterloo express, 9 September 1959. (J.M. Bentley/John Scott-Morgan Collection)

31860 at Barnstaple Junction with the 3.58pm WR empty stock train for Taunton, 26 May 1961. (MLS Collection)

31857 runs alongside the River Camel at Padstow with the portion of a Waterloo bound express, 8 August 1962. (MLS Collection)

Two 'N's awaiting departure from Ilfracombe, 31838 and 31845, 1963. (Lens of Sutton/John Scott-Morgan Collection)

31836 ready to depart with a passenger train from Bude to Exeter Central, 19 July 1963. (E.W. Fry/John Scott-Morgan Collection)

31854 leaving Eridge,
14 October 1961.
(David Clark)

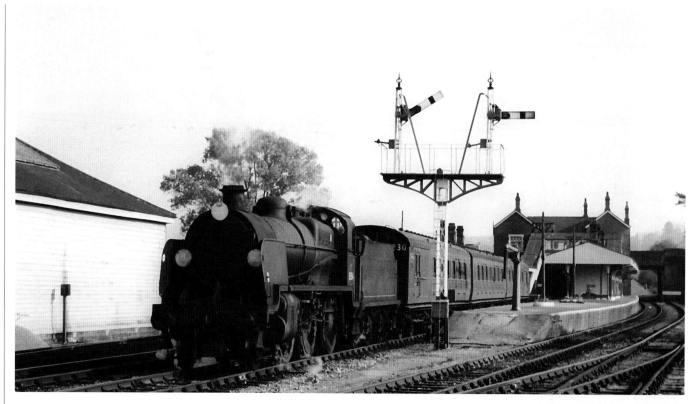

31871 near Eridge,
17 March 1962.
(David Clark)

31823 passes through East Grinstead (High Level) with a freight, 31 August 1962.
(David Clark)

31402 departing Shalford with a Reading-Redhill train, July 1961.
(Ken Wightman)

31872 shuts off steam ready to stop at Shalford station with a Reading-Redhill train, July 1961. (Ken Wightman)

31403 departing from Betchworth with a Redhill-Reading train, 12 August 1961. (David Clark)

31851 plus a second 'N' on an evening Redhill-Reading train at Reigate, July 1962. (Roy Hobbs/Online Transport Archive)

An unidentified 'N' on a South Coast Midlands inter-regional holiday express approaching Redhill Tunnel, August 1962. (Roy Hobbs/Online Transport Archive)

31863 on an excursion for the Western Region at Gomshall, 25 August 1962. (Ken Wightman)

31867 near Bough Beech with a Tonbridge-Redhill-Reading train, August 1962. (Ken Wightman)

31868, with renewed frame front end, near Chilworth with a Redhill-Reading train, August 1962. (Ken Wightman)

31411 at Nutfield with a Redhill-Tonbridge train, June 1963. (Roy Hobbs/ Online Transport Archive)

31405 between Reigate and Betchworth with a train for Guildford, October 1964. (Roy Hobbs/ Online Transport Archive)

31816 passing through Winchester City with an up boat train from Lymington Pier, 11 August 1962. (Colin Boocock)

31405 with renewed front end pilots BR '4' 2-6-4T 80139 at Ash Junction with a Redhill-Reading train, 3 October 1964. (Rodney Lissenden)

31816 at Winnersh Halt on the Reading-Guildford route, 29 July 1964. (MLS Collection)

31821 leaving Salisbury with a freight for Basingstoke, 27 August 1963. (Rodney Lissenden)

31408 passes West Weybridge & New Haw near the former Brooklands racing track with a van train from Nine Elms, 12 March 1964. (Rodney Lissenden)

31843 on a two-coach portion of a Waterloo express at Halwill Junction, 6 May 1963. (John Scott-Morgan Collection)

31840 shunts wagons at Boscarne Junction, 4 May 1964. (Roy Hobbs /Online Transport Archive)

31406 shunts a set of LMR coaches at Ilfracombe ready for a GW mogul to take a returning holiday express to the West Midlands, which the SR mogul will bank to Mortehoe summit, 25 July 1964. (J.H. Aston/John Scott-Morgan Collection)

31411 with the *Sussex Downsman* RCTS/LCGB railtour on Falmer Bank, 22 March 1964. (Roy Hobbs/Online Transport Archive)

Two 'N's on Exmouth Junction depot, 31842 and 31834, 30 June 1964. (N.K. Harrop/MLS Collection)

Preservation
31874

31874 was built in 1925 at Woolwich Arsenal, and was provided with a new front end to the frames, new cylinders and outside steam pipes in May 1957. It was withdrawn in March 1964, when based in the Western Region's Plymouth Division at Exmouth Junction. It was sold to Woodham Brothers and was towed to Barry where it was stored derelict with the vast Barry collection of condemned locomotives awaiting scrapping until purchased by the Mid Hants Preservation Society and moved to Alresford in March 1974. It was repaired and restored to traffic over the following three years and painted BR mixed traffic lined black livery and named *Aznar Line,* in gratitude to the Spanish shipping company that sponsored its road movement from Barry to Alresford. It commenced operations between Alresford and Ropley at the end of April 1977, and was renamed *Brian Fisk* after the husband of one of the major donors. It was withdrawn finally in 1998 with severe firebox problems and then stood out of service for sixteen years, unlikely to be repaired, until moved in 2014 to the Swanage Railway where a major general overhaul involving complete stripping down to the main frame has taken place. In May 2016, an inspection of the work indicated that main line

The condemned 31874 at Barry Scrapyard from whence it was rescued in 1974. It lies rotting in the company of two 'Halls' and a GW 56XX 0-6-2T. (MLS Collection)

The resurrected 31874, named *Aznar Line* after the shipping company that sponsored its transfer to Alresford, at that station after working the 6.5pm train from Ropley, 16 September 1978. (MLS Collection)

certification would be sought once the restoration was complete – the process still ongoing in 2017.

Personal Reminiscences of the 'N's

My experience of the Southern Region 'N' 2-6-0s was limited to three distinct phases of my railway enthusiast career. I was at school in Surbiton from 1949 to 1951 and although I saw a wide variety of South Western motive power after school every day, it was not until I got a Surrey County Council scholarship to Charterhouse, near Godalming, that I saw the 'N' class with any frequency. I would cycle to Wanborough or Shalford, either side of Guildford, trainspotting until I was about fourteen, and afterwards trying out my camera skills. Mostly it was the larger wheeled 'U' moguls that ran the passenger service on the Reading-Redhill services that I saw, but an occasional 'N' would turn up and one of the less frequent freights would certainly be 'N' hauled. Then after I left school, but still lived in the area (Woking), I met them more often on the Reading-Redhill passenger services as they lasted to 1964-5, rather than the 'U's, most of which were withdrawn in 1962-3. I particularly remember engines like 31858 and 31862-31866, which became very common round the Guildford area in the last few months before DMUs took over the route in January 1965.

The second area where I came across them was on the Southern's North Devon and Cornwall services, breaking the monotony from the Bulleid light pacifics which seemed to dominate everything else apart from a tantalising snip behind a 'T9'. A fortnight's summer holiday in Ilfracombe in August 1956 was my first opportunity to savour this experience and I took full advantage of it. I took the camera out several times up to Mortehoe while the rest of the family found the beach, and tried to choose a mogul rather than a 'West Country' to ride behind as I was very used to the latter at home. I had one opportunity to get a shot of a freight with 31830 bowling along at the top of the bank. On the middle summer Saturday, the 11th, I decided to walk from Mortehoe to Braunton along country lanes near the line and find suitable places to photograph trains working hard up the bank. Unfortunately, it was a beautiful hot summer's day – good for walking but not for photography as the heat evaporated the trains' exhaust, so even though working hard, the pacifics especially just exhibited a light haze. My train out of Ilfracombe was a heavy holiday express for the West Midlands hauled by WR mogul 7311, but banked to Mortehoe by an 'N' that had brought the empty stock in. I photographed a succession of pacifics, but one 'N', 31837, broke the monotony and was seen charging up the bank with a string of LSWR coaches on a semi-fast from Yeovil Junction.

The third phase of my contact with this class was an occasional encounter whilst commuting to London University and weekend sorties to the lineside around Woking and then after I joined British Railways in 1960, I had access to cheap quarter-fare 'privilege tickets', which enabled me to search out steam in my spare time in the early 1960s. In particular, after starting the Western Region's management training scheme, I spent much of the first year (September 1961 to March 1962) based at Reading, and although I had a B&B there,

31874 with a Reading-Redhill train at Shalford, May 1956. (David Maidment)

31830 runs a freight bound for Ilfracombe near Mortehoe, at the top of the bank from Braunton, 8 August 1956. (David Maidment)

31837 climbing Braunton bank to Mortehoe with a Yeovil Junction-Ilfracombe train, 11 August 1956. (David Maidment)

'N' 31813 with a ballast train on the down fast just west of Woking Junction, 2 April 1958. (David Maidment)

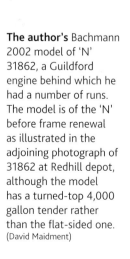

The author's Bachmann 2002 model of 'N' 31862, a Guildford engine behind which he had a number of runs. The model is of the 'N' before frame renewal as illustrated in the adjoining photograph of 31862 at Redhill depot, although the model has a turned-top 4,000 gallon tender rather than the flat-sided one. (David Maidment)

31862, of which the author has a model, at Redhill depot where it was allocated, before frame renewal in April 1960, seen here c1958. (MLS Collection)

I spent evenings travelling around when not on shift work. Whilst most of my travels were to Paddington, Oxford or Swindon, I did make a number of trips on the Reading Southern line towards Wokingham and Guilford, and I often travelled to and from home at weekends changing between the Farnborough stations, or going via Guildford. Then in the autumn of 1962 and the first half of 1963 I was training in South Wales and after the main London-Swansea trains were dieselised in the summer of 1962, I tried other ways to make the journey to incorporate some steam work, and the Guildford-Reading route featured frequently

in this. As well as a few 'U's, I also garnered some 'N' haulage during this period, particularly the 314xx series (I had runs behind 31400, 31402, 31410, 31411 (2 runs), 31413 and 31414, as well as the 31862-66 group I mentioned earlier). On three coach stopping services on this line they were never really extended, but conducted their work efficiently enough, although most of the 'N's towards the end finished in a pretty filthy state.

I have a fairly large collection of 'OO' and 'HO' models, UK and continental, and currently my layout hosts the SR scene of the late 1950s and early 1960s. This includes a number of the classes

described in this book and I'm including a couple of photos of the appropriate models, many of which have come onto the scene only this century as more and more variety is introduced and quality (and prices) have increased. I have to admit that I never remember even seeing a 3-cylinder 'N1'. I acquired secondhand a fairly basic kit made model of a 3-cylinder mogul back in the 1980s, which I had always assumed to be a 'U1', but when I got it out for photographing, I saw when I really scrutinised it under the anonymous black paint crudely applied before I bought it (for £20) the outline of the number 31876, so therefore learned that the builder

The author's model of 'N1' 31876, which was acquired secondhand in 1986. It is a kit built Wills Finecast body on a Triang chassis. (David Maidment)

was intending to model an 'N1'. One of the tasks awaiting me is to airbrush the bodywork properly and restore its correct identity.

The 3-Cylinder 'N1'

Harold Holcroft had designed a conjugated valve gear for three-cylinder locomotives when employed at Swindon in 1913 and although Churchward had no intention of building a three-cylinder engine for the GWR, he encouraged Holcroft to seek a patent for the design. When Gresley developed his conjugated gear for the 'O2' 2-8-0, which was subject to some criticism, he approached Holcroft, who had given a well-received paper about his valve gear patent to the Institute of Locomotive Engineers, and as a result Gresley simplified his

gear design for the 'K3' mogul he designed for the GNR. Holcroft had been recruited as part of Maunsell's new team at Ashford, and the latter encouraged his assistant in early 1919 to produce a design for a three-cylinder version of the 1917 'N' (and also the 'K' 2-6-4T – see next chapter). Holcroft had the drawings ready by June 1920 and one example of both the mogul and passenger tank engine were ordered. The 'N1' as it was classified was developed from the thirteenth 'N' to be constructed, 822, and it was completed and first steamed on 19 March 1923.

The key differences from the two-cylinder 'N' were: three 16in x 28in diameter cylinders, 190lb psi boiler pressure instead of 200lb, and increased engine weight of 62 tons 15 cwt, with higher axleload of 18½

tons. The chimney was slightly larger in diameter and the boiler was 3in higher pitched. The engine had two sets of Walschaerts valve gear for the outside cylinders and Holcroft's derived gear for the inside cylinder.

822 commenced tests immediately on van and empty stock trains and on a Hither Green-Paddock Wood freight turn. Then, when these passed successfully, it operated from Bricklayers Arms on freight and semi-fast passenger turns. In the autumn of 1923, it was tested in comparison with 'N's 810 and 817 and was slightly more economical (66.7lb of coal per mile compared with 69.3 and 70.2 of the other two), and was found to give a much superior ride at higher speeds on passenger trains. With full regulator and shorter cut-offs than was used on the 'N', it rode smoothly and

822

SECR

A **works** photograph of the 3-cylinder 'N1' prototype, March 1923. (Loco Publishing Co./ MLS Collection)

on later tests for the Bridge Stress Committee, it was timed successfully at a maximum speed of 79mph.

822 first appeared in the SE&CR wartime grey livery, but at its first general overhaul in 1925 it was repainted in SR lined green. There had been some problems with the Holcroft valve gear, especially when travelling at speed as its mileage rose and maintenance standards were suspect, but this did not prevent the SR management ordering five more 'N1's in March 1928 at a cost of £8,940 each. They utilised frames

and some parts purchased from Woolwich Arsenal in 1925 and assembly began in November 1929, with A876 and A877 appearing from Ashford in March 1930, A878 and A879 in April and A880 in May. However, because of the problems experienced with the derived gear in general traffic, these five engines were fitted with three sets of conventional Walschaerts gear. They also received a standard 'N' chimney, had 200lb psi boiler pressure and larger 4,000 gallon tenders weighing 42 tons 8cwt. 822 also received

Walschaerts valve gear for the inside cylinders as well as a renewal of all three cylinders. All were renumbered as 1822 and 1876-1880 in 1931.

1822 remained at Bricklayers Arms, but the new engines were allocated to New Cross Gate for Central Section main line freights and weekend excursions, and on the Hastings route where the 2-cylinder 'N's were banned through the restricted kinetic envelope of Bo Peep and Mountfield tunnels. After electrification of the Brighton route, 1878-1880 went to Eastbourne for main line goods work and passenger trains from the South Coast to the LMS via Kensington and Willesden at weekends. 1822, 1879 and 1880 were transferred to Tonbridge in October 1935 and 1876-1878 to Bricklayers Arms. They all received smoke deflectors around this time. In 1938, 1879 and 1880 were allocated to Stewarts Lane. During the Second World War, all moved to Tonbridge for wartime freight and troop movement, with 1822, 1876 and 1880 on loan to St Leonards in 1943-4 for the build-up to D-Day. After the war, all were reallocated to Hither Green for freight work and regular haulage of the 5.40pm Cannon Street-Ashford commuter train, on which they attained a good reputation

for reliability and punctuality. In June 1946, 1822, 1876 and 1877 again returned to Tonbridge and at nationalisation all were renumbered and repainted in the BR mixed traffic lined black livery although this did not start until June 1949 (31877) and be completed until November 1954 (31878).

They were replaced at Tonbridge by the Bulleid 'Q1' 0-6-0s in mid-1949 and 1822, 1876 and 1877 went to St Leonards for haulage of gypsum trains. Three were found to be unnecessary and 31877 was sent to Hither Green, where its 'N1's regularly worked the 12noon Victoria-Margate and 4.23pm Margate-Victoria on summer Saturdays. 31822 and 31876 were replaced at

St Leonards by 'Q1's despite crew protests (the 'N1's were popular and had better braking capacity than the 0-6-0s). All six engines were now at Hither Green on main line freight work.

In June 1959 the 'N1's returned to Tonbridge for goods train action on the Hastings line and semi-fast and local passenger work to Ashford, Brighton and Redhill. They were replaced as diesels became available for freight work in May 1962, and finished their days at Stewarts Lane before mass withdrawal of the class in November 1962. 31822 as the oldest member had 859,851 miles to its credit, the lowest mileage being 714,823 run by 31879.

1878 at its home depot of Hither Green, still in wartime black Southern Railway livery five months after nationalisation, 21 May 1948. (MLS Collection)

31880 at Ashford in BR mixed traffic lined black livery but without the 'lion & wheel' logo on the tender, 6 September 1952. (MLS Collection)

31876 still in wartime black livery at Shortlands (Downs Bridge) with a Victoria-Ramsgate relief express in the summer of 1954. (Ken Wightman)

31876 in the final BR mixed traffic livery at Hither Green, 13 October 1956. (MLS Collection)

31822, the 1923 built prototype 'N1', at Hither Green depot, October 1958. (MLS Collection)

31876 in BR mixed traffic lined livery departs from Tonbridge with a stopping train to Ashford, 17 August 1957. (Ken Wightman)

31877 at Tonbridge shed, 23 May 1959. (MLS Collection)

31877 in the company of an unidentified 'Schools' at Tonbridge depot, 23 May 1959. (MLS Collection)

31876 in ex-works condition at St Mary Cray on an empty coaching stock train for the Kent Coast, 16 May 1959. (R.C. Riley)

With third rails already in place, 31878 enters Paddock Wood with a Victoria-Kent Coast relief express, 10 June 1961. (David Clark)

31822 leaving Redhill with a train for Guildford and Reading, 7 October 1961. (Colin Boocock)

Other 'Woolwich' locomotives
The Metropolitan 2-6-4Ts

The Metropolitan Railway needed extra power for its developing freight work, and to increase the freight train loads to reduce the number of freight paths between the frequent electric passenger trains south of Rickmansworth. In 1924, its most powerful goods locomotives were 0-6-2Ts. The management specified the need for an engine capable of hauling 600 tons at 35mph or climbing the 1 in 94 gradient in the Chilterns at 25mph. At that time, the Woolwich Arsenal was advertising the moguls it had built to maintain its workforce and the Metropolitan's Chief Mechanical Engineer contracted Armstrong Whitworth & Co to

The first 2-6-4T for the Metropolitan Railway still in works grey at Armstrong Whitworth's Works at Newcastle prior to delivery and painting in Metropolitan livery, January 1925. (MLS Collection)

Metropolitan 2-6-4T 111 with passenger 4-4-4T 110 at Neasden, March 1925. (MLS Collection)

Two photos of 2-6-4T 113 just after delivery at Neasden, March 1925. (Real Photographs/ MLS Collection)

convert and assemble six of these as 2-6-4 tank engines at a cost of £5,000 each, £13,000 for the parts for the six locomotives plus a spare boiler and £3,000 for the assembly of each locomotive – a significantly reduced price as the government was desperate to sell the surplus engines. The first completed locomotive, Metropolitan Railway No.111, was completed in January 1925 and was in traffic by March. All six had been completed by mid-February and delivered into traffic by the end of March. They were identified as class 'K' in the Metropolitan stock.

Principal dimensions of the engines were: 2 cylinders 19in x 28in, Walschaerts valve gear, 5ft 6in coupled wheels, 3ft 1in bogie and pony truck wheels, 200lb psi boiler pressure, 1,810sqft heating surface, 25sqft grate area, 2,000 gallons water capacity (500 gallons in each side tank, 1,000 gallons below the coal space) and 4 tons of coal. Weight was 87 tons 7cwt and tractive effort 26,100lb. The livery was a deep red, a little darker than the Midland Railway livery, lined in black and yellow. In many ways they were very similar in dimensions and purpose to the Southern Railway's 'W' class of 2-6-4Ts.

The engines operated almost exclusively on freight trains between Verney Junction, Aylesbury, Rickmansworth and Harrow, but were not allowed through the Finchley tunnels. They were capable of operating passenger trains but the Metropolitan Railway had eight 'H' class 4-4-4Ts for this purpose. London Transport absorbed the Metropolitan Railway in July 1933 and the engines received the London Transport livery.

In 1937, Neasden Works and depot was rebuilt and the steam shed demolished and as a result agreement was reached to transfer responsibility for freight and passenger work on the non-electrified section north of Rickmansworth to the LNER. The 'K' class 2-6-4Ts together with some other class 'G' and 'H' engines were sold to the LNER and operated from the former Great Central depot at Neasden. Works overhauls were carried out at Stratford.

116 in London Transport livery after absorption of the Metropolitan Railway into the London Transport network, at Neasden, 11 July 1936. (H.C. Casserley/J.M. Bentley Collection)

116 with a Verney Junction – London freight, c1927. (LCGB/K. Nunn/John Scott-Morgan Collection)

113 with a freight near Wendover, c1928. (J.M. Bentley Collection)

116 bunker first near Wendover with a freight bound for London, c1928. (John Scott-Morgan Collection)

112 in London Transport livery with a freight at ChorleyWood, 17 August 1935. (H.C. Casserley/ J.M. Bentley Collection)

LNER 6159 (former Met 112) at Neasden, 18 February 1939. 6159 was withdrawn in 1943 before receiving the later LNER number. (L.B. Lapper/ J.M. Bentley Collection)

LNER 6162 (ex Met 115) on a freight train at Waddesden, between Quainton Road and Aylesbury, 17 June 1939. (H.C. Casserley/J.M. Bentley Collection)

LNER 6160 (ex Met 113) at Rickmansworth with an Aylesbury-Baker Street train, with LT 0-4-4T No.L48 in the bay platform, 27 April 1946. The LNER 'L2' tanks were rarely seen on passenger work although in the immediate post-war period they could be pressed into service as here during other power shortages. (H.C. Casserley/J.M. Bentley Collection)

6160 at Neasden awaiting repair in a line with another former Met tank and a Great Central withdrawn 4-6-0, 6 June 1946. Despite appearances, 6160 was repaired and renumbered 9071 and was not withdrawn until 1947. (H.C. Casserley/J.M. Bentley Collection)

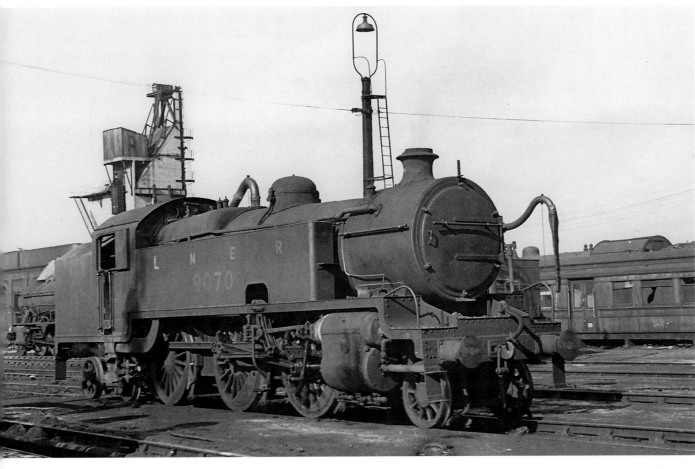

Under LNER ownership, 9070 (ex Met 111 and early LNER No. 6158) at Neasden, 23 June 1948. It was one of the last two, withdrawn in October that year.
(H.C. Casserley/J.M. Bentley Collection)

Ex Metropolitan 2-6-4T 113, now 'L2' LNER 9071 (still with pre-1946 number 6160 on the bufferbeam) at Aylesbury with a freight, c1947.
(John Scott-Morgan Collection)

Ex-Met tank 113, renumbered 6160, then 9071 in 1946, seen here at Stratford Works, 4 June 1947. Although it looks as though it may be withdrawn, it was not in fact condemned until October the following year. (H.C. Casserley/ J.M. Bentley Collection)

During the war, some passenger turns were hauled by the 'L2's as the 'K' tank engines were now classified in the LNER system. They were painted unlined black and renumbered 6158-6163, but 6159 (ex 112) and 6161 (ex 114) were withdrawn in 1943. The others were allocated 9070-9073 in the LNER 1946 renumbering scheme, but only 9070 (ex 111) and 9071 (ex 113) carried these numbers, the other two being withdrawn in 1945 (ex 116) and 1946 (ex 115). The remaining two were condemned in October 1948 and never received BR numbers or livery. The average mileage of the six locomotives was 287,300, only a third of that of the comparable SR 'W' tanks.

The Irish 2-6-0s ('K1' and 'K1a')

In March 1923, the Irish Midland and Great Western Railway (Dublin-Galway, Athlone-Westport and Mullingar-Sligo) ordered twelve sets of parts from the Woolwich Arsenal at a cost of £24,000 and Broadstone Works, Dublin, was about to commence the assembly work when that company was absorbed by the Great Southern Railway (GSR). The completed moguls converted to the Irish gauge of 5ft 3in were ready and entered service between April 1925 and March 1927, numbered 372-383.

The newly amalgamated company had inherited 587 locomotives in 114 classes, many examples just single or pairs. The GSR therefore acquired a further fifteen sets of parts and four spare boilers for £34,000 and the first eight, also with 5ft 6in diameter coupled wheels, entered service numbered 384-391 between October 1927 and June 1929. All bore the GSR grey livery. A ninth set was retained for spares. These locomotives were classified as 'K1' 2-6-0s. Because of their origin at Woolwich and the fact that they had been acquired at 'knock-down' prices, they were nicknamed 'Woolworths'.

The principal dimensional differences to the SR 'N's were: total heating surface, 1,811sqft, weight 61 tons (with tender 100 tons 5cwt) and tractive effort, 26,000lb. The remaining six sets of parts received 6ft diameter coupled wheels and were built between July and December 1930, as class 'K1a', and numbered 393-398. These had small splashers like the 'River' rebuilds on the Southern (see next chapter) and a raised boiler height of 3in.

The GSR was amalgamated with the Dublin United Tramways Company as the *Coras Iompair Eireann* (CIE) on 1 January 1945, and nationalised in 1950, but both these classes retained their previous GSR numbers. There was a critical coal situation in 1947-8, when experiments were made with alternative fuel, including Bulleid's turf-burning locomotives, but 30-40 engines were converted to oil-burning using the Weir system by March 1947, with eventually 93 in total, including many of the 372 and 393 moguls. They bore a large white circle painted on the smokebox door and either side of the tender to indicate to signalmen that they were oil-burners. The tests with a 372 ('K1') class between Cork and Kingsbridge demonstrated a saving of 60 tons of coal per week, but by 1948, the coal situation had improved and the locomotives were reconverted to coal-burning.

They operated on both passenger and goods traffic on the former GSR and M&GWR main lines and on the Mallow-Tralee branch, as well as goods trains on the Waterford-Dublin and Waterford-Limerick routes.

'K1' 374 , a Woolwich Arsenal 'Woolworth' 2-6-0 with 5ft 6in coupled wheels, purchased by the Great Southern & Western Railway of Ireland , c1926. (W.A. Camwell/ MLS Collection)

378, 'K1' 2-6-0, c1928 after construction from Woolwich Arsenal parts. (W.A. Camwell/MLS Collection)

394, a 'K1a' 2-6-0 with 6ft 0in coupled wheels, purchased from Woolwich Arsenal and assembled by the GSR in 1930, photographed in 1931. (Railway Photographs/ MLS Collection)

'K1' 373 ex works at Inchicore, in CIE livery, c1948. (W.A. Camwell/ MLS Collection)

'K1' 383 at Broadstone depot, Dublin, June 1956. (Colin Boocock)

'K1' 384 at Cork Glanmire Road, 3 July 1955. (MLS Collection)

'K1a' 396 and a further 'Woolworth' mogul at Inchicore, 19 August 1955. (A.C. Gilbert/ MLS Collection)

'K1a' 396 at Broadstone depot, Dublin, June 1956.
(Colin Boocock)

'K1' 378 and a further 'K1' at Broadstone depot, Dublin, c1958.
(MLS Collection)

'K1' 373 on the 8.30am Dublin Westland Row-Galway train, 16 August 1955. (A.C. Gilbert/MLS Collection)

A doubleheaded mail train, the 3.30pm Galway-Dublin Westland Row, hauled by 'K1' 373 and piloted by 'J19' 0-6-0 599 at Mullingar, 15 August 1955. (MLS Collection)

'K1' 385 on arrival at Killarney with the 9.30am from Cork and Mallow to Tralee, 17 August 1955. (A.C. Gilbert/MLS Collection)

'K1a' 393 at Mullingar with a Sligo-Dublin train, c1955. (W.A. Camwell/ MLS Collection)

'K1a' 396 at Athenry with a Galway-Dublin train, c1955. (W.A. Camwell/ MLS Collection)

They were invariably in charge of the mail trains and expresses on the Galway route and the fastest trains covered the 52½ miles between Mullingar and Dublin in both directions in 75 minutes. They were also dominant on the Cork-Rosslare Harbour trains. They sometimes had problems on heavy freights through lack of sufficient brake power and there were a number of runaway incidents, the most serious being at Cahir where No.375 and 32 wagons on a beet train from Waterford to Thurles finished up in the River Suir, killing her crew.

The 'K1a's with their 6ft driving wheels were used on fast passenger trains and have been timed up to 75mph (as were the 5ft 6in engines on occasions). In the 1930s, one of them is rumoured to have brought the 'Steel Train' (flush-panelled stock for the Cork Mail, 240 tons) from Cork to Dublin, with two stops, 165 miles, in 159 minutes running time.

All the locomotives were useful mixed traffic engines and survived until near the end of steam, being withdrawn between 1954 and 1962, including 375 at the end of 1955 as the result of the Cahir runaway accident. They were hard riding engines, prone to roughness, and normally were excellent 'steamers', despite occasional lapses.

Chapter 3

THE 'K'S & 'K1' ('RIVER' CLASS 2-6-4T)

Design & Construction

One of the key members of staff that Maunsell had recruited to his office at Ashford in 1913 was James Clayton, who left the Midland at Derby to become Chief Locomotive Draughtsman of the South Eastern & Chatham Railway. He had just been involved in the design of a large 2-6-4T with Henry Fowler to replace the Whitelegg 4-6-4Ts on the London Tilbury and Southend Railway (which in fact were not built) and Clayton and Pearson, the Assistant Chief Mechanical Engineer enticed away from Swindon, obtained drawings of this and advocated a similar design for the South Eastern expresses, since the length of journeys in Kent was considered to be well within the range of a large tank engine. In fact, the Whitelegg tank engines had been offered to the South Eastern Railway in 1912 and the Locomotive Committee had been keen to take them. One had been loaned and both Wainwright and his Chief Draughtsman, Robert Surtees, rode on it but concluded that it rode unsteadily and vetoed

it – a warning that perhaps their successors at Ashford should have heeded.

Maunsell had set about planning five standard classes to try to thin out the myriad different types of locomotives he inherited and the maintenance problems that such a wide number of types caused. Top of his priorities were a freight engine (the 'N' class described in the previous chapter) and an express passenger locomotive to deal with increased loads and the need to accelerate trains to the Kent ports and coastal resorts. Maunsell disagreed with Pearson and Clayton, who advocated a similar 2-6-4 tank engine whilst he favoured developing the reasonably successful 'L' 4-4-0 that he had modified from the Wainwright design and had built in 1914 as a matter of urgency. However, the improvements that Maunsell envisaged – higher boiler pressure, outside cylinders, superheater and Walschaerts valve gear – took the weight over that permitted by the civil engineer and so Maunsell was persuaded to explore and develop the Pearson/Clayton proposal. He satisfied himself that an express

tank engine within the axleweight limits imposed was a practicable proposition and instructed drawings to be prepared.

The coupled wheels were to be 6ft in diameter (compared with the proposed Midland 2-6-4T of 6ft 3in) but a higher boiler pressure of 200lb psi (instead of the Midland 175). Pearson and Maunsell were both well aware of the moves to higher boiler pressures pioneered by Churchward on the Great Western. With a Maunsell superheater, total heating surface would be 1,850sqft, the grate area 25sqft and with tanks holding 2,000 gallons and a 2½ ton capacity bunker, the axleload was kept to an acceptable 18½ tons over the centre coupled wheels, the engine weight being 82 tons 5cwt. The boiler was domeless, following GWR practice – though what appeared to be a dome was in fact the casing for topfeed and external clackboxes. Maunsell had now realised the merit of the GWR long valve travel arrangements and provided a generous 67/8in travel with a lap of 1½in and a lead of ¾in unlike his previous decision to reduce the valve travel on the Wainwright 'L' which he seems to have acknowledged to be a mistake. The frames were not as robust as some previous SE&CR designs, in order to save weight, a significant problem in later years after their conversion to moguls. The proposals were put before the directors in January 1915 and the construction of six class 'K' 2-6-4Ts was authorised.

With the war pressures continuing, it was 1917 before the first examples of both the 'N' 2-6-0 and 'K' were constructed and despite the larger order, only one of each class was built, the rest delayed until trials had been completed and the war ended. The 'K' prototype, No.790, emerged from Ashford Works in June 1917 and failed on its first test run to Headcorn, with firebox problems and faulty lubrication. After adjustments, 790 entered regular service operating from Bricklayers Arms shed in July 1917. It was turned out in the wartime grey livery with the white number painted on the side tanks and a small plate indicating SECR on the bunker.

Initial trials between Cannon Street and Folkestone Junction were concluded successfully from a performance point of view and whilst the coal capacity was more than adequate, there were concerns about the safety margin on water consumption, and it was decreed that the 2-6-4T could only be used on Folkestone expresses if there was a stop at Ashford during which the water supply could be topped up. In fact, its early regular diagram included two Folkestone expresses, one of which was the up morning Pullman train, but both stopped at Tonbridge where drivers were

The prototype 'K' 2-6-4T immediately after construction at Ashford, with its designer, Richard Maunsell, standing alongside, June 1917. (Locomotive Publishing Co./ MLS Collection)

instructed to take on water. There were teething problems concerning the mechanical lubrication and sanding apparatus, which were later modified, arrangements carried over to the rest of the class when built in 1925.

In 1922, No.790 was reallocated to Tonbridge and undertook fast commuter services to and from London via Redhill, but the track between Tonbridge and Redhill was poor and the heavy tank engine caused problems, so it was returned to Bricklayers Arms later in the year and was restricted to semi-fast services to Dover via Sevenoaks and Ashford. In the autumn of 1922, Maunsell instructed staff to carry out some comparative tests between the 'L' 4-4-0, a 'D1' rebuild 4-4-0 and 790. Harry Holcroft rode on the engines and reported that there was little

to choose between the 'L' and the 'K', the 4-4-0 having the superior boiler and the 'K' the better cylinder efficiency (apparently the 'D1' was better than either). Holcroft also reported that, on the whole, 790 ran smoothly and had a very comfortable cab, but when it hit a weakness in the track (loose joint or soft spot) the engine rolled heavily – a sign that perhaps should have caused more concern.

More 'K's had been ordered in 1920 at a projected cost of £5,380, but with certain parts from Woolwich to hasten construction, boilers being ordered from the North British Locomotive Company for the same reason. However, despite the apparent haste, it was 1924 before all the various parts were assembled at Ashford for construction to commence. The engines were

required for the 1925 summer service and as Ashford could not guarantee this, the firm of Armstrong Whitworth assembled nine of the sets of parts. The nine engines were duly delivered between February and May 1925 and numbered A791-A799, were painted in Southern Railway lined green livery and named according to the Railway's policy for engines engaged in passenger work – in this case after rivers that flowed through the company's territory:

A791 *River Adur*
A792 *River Arun*
A793 *River Ouse*
A794 *River Rother*
A795 *River Medway*
A796 *River Stour*
A797 *River Mole*
A798 *River Wey*
A799 *River Test*

The lone pioneer 'K' now joined by a further nine of the first order, repainted in Southern Railway green livery and named *River Avon*, c1925. (Photomatic/John Scott-Morgan Collection)

A791 *River Adur* c1926.
(Lens of Sutton/John Scott-Morgan Collection)

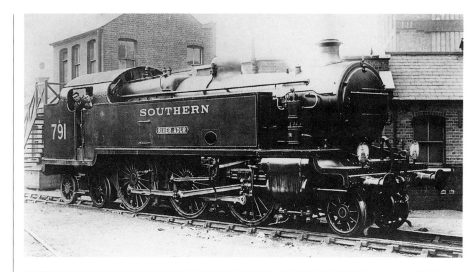

A792 *River Arun*
at Brighton, c1926.
(John Scott-Morgan Collection)

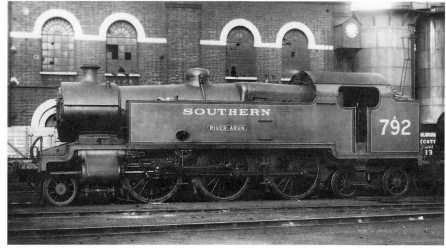

A793 *River Ouse* at
Eastbourne, c1926.
(MLS Collection)

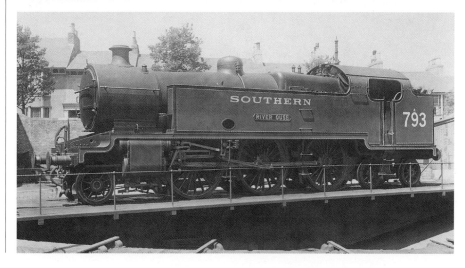

At the same time A790 received the name *River Avon*.

Certain developments took place between the building of A790 and the 1925 batch. The degree of superheating was increased and a conventional dome was included as well as a steam sander and sight feed lubricator. In addition to the vacuum brake, these nine engines were also equipped with the Westinghouse brake, the air pump being placed on the right-hand side of the smokebox. A790 was also dual brake fitted at the same time.

There were complaints of poor riding during the summer and alterations were made to the springing of A790. A further ten locomotives were built at Brighton Works in 1926 which incorporated the modifications made to A790. The new batch of locomotives was numbered A800-A809 and named as follows:

A800 *River Cray*
A801 *River Darenth*
A802 *River Cuckmere*
A803 *River Itchen*
A804 *River Tamar*
A805 *River Camel*
A806 *River Torridge*
A807 *River Axe*
A808 *River Char*
A809 *River Dart*

The modifications and slight increase in tank capacity (just under 2,100 gallons) increased the weight to 84 tons and axleload to 18 tons 15cwt.

Again, there were complaints about poor riding, especially of a couple of the 1925 batch, and tests were made on the London-Brighton route where the inspector found the riding similar to that of the LBSCR 4-6-2Ts but inferior to the 'Baltics'. Despite this, twenty more 'K's had been authorised in March 1926 to be built at Brighton, allocated numbers from A610 to A629. The Locomotive Running Department had some reservations about this, but Ashford had built the frames and cast the cylinders before circumstances changed dramatically.

In the meantime, the tenth set of parts assembled at Ashford remained there, and a 3-cylinder version was built at the Works in 1925, being delivered at the beginning of December. Holcroft had designed a derived valve gear arrangement for a 3-cylinder locomotive when still on the GWR and although Churchward did not build any 3-cylinder engines, he encouraged Holcroft to patent it. Gresley was interested in that it was a simpler design than that initially used on his 3-cylinder engines and Maunsell was concerned that Gresley was trying to entice his man away from the Southern. He therefore took interest in Holcroft's design and agreed to test it out on this tenth 2-6-4T of the 1925 order, and A890 emerged classified class 'K1' and named *River Frome*. It had three 16in x 28in cylinders, but other dimensions were similar to the 2-cylinder engines. It weighed 88 tons 15cwt and had a heavier axleload of 19 tons 5cwt. It was very similar to the sole 3-cylinder 'N1' (A822) in many respects, basically a tank engine version.

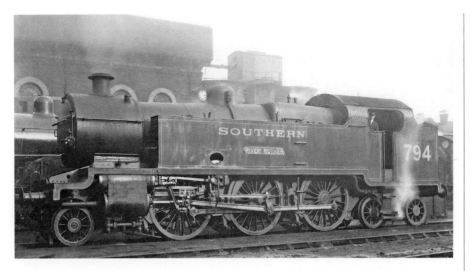

A794 *River Rother*, c1927. (Real Photographs/John Scott-Morgan Collection)

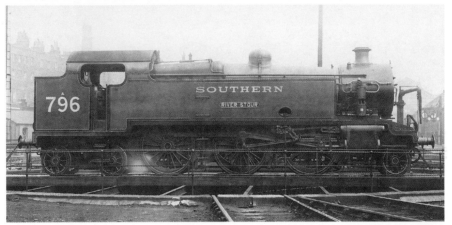

A796 *River Stour* at Brighton, c1926. (Real Photographs/John Scott-Morgan Collection)

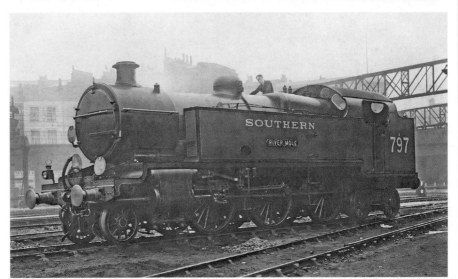

A797 *River Mole* at Victoria, c1926. (MLS Collection)

A803 *River Itchen* , one of the second batch of 'Rivers' at Redhill, ready for action, 2 October 1926. (H.C. Casserley/John Scott-Morgan Collection)

3-cylinder A890 *River Frome* as built in Works grey, 1925. (John Scott-Morgan Collection)

A890 did not have the springing modifications made to A790 and adopted for the 1926 Brighton built engines and it received complaints of poor riding similar to members of the 'K' class. In March 1927, A890 derailed at speed, luckily without fatalities or too much damage and the inquiry blamed faulty track elevation. During the repairs to the engine, the springing modifications were implemented. Another derailment on a curve took place in August 1927 and the inspecting officer again found fault with the track. The company did not seem to realise the effect of the heavy express tank engines on the track and their vulnerability when

encountering insufficient ballasting, soft spots or poor drainage. Much of the ballast used up to 1918 was shingle recovered from the beaches near Dungeness, but the pebbles worn smooth by the sea did not have the same grip as rough stone and the SECR changed its supply, but there were still many sections of track laid on shingle and sand, easily affected by bad weather, especially heavy rain.

However, these accidents concerned the Board and a number of directors wished to have the 'K's and the 'K1' banned from main line passenger work, a proposal rejected by the Chairman just before the final disastrous accident to A800

and its train on 24 August 1927, when approaching Sevenoaks at around 55-60mph on the 5pm Cannon Street-Deal Pullman car express. Thirteen people were killed and all the 2-6-4Ts were removed from traffic pending the outcome of the inquiry. As part of the investigations, A803 and A890 were sent for trials on the LNER main line, where both engines rode well at speeds in excess of 80mph – but this was one of the best stretches of track in the country. A 'King Arthur' also took part (E782 *Sir Brian*) and was even more impressive than the tank engines, though it was subject to vibration. Tests were then carried out on the Southern

A890 *River Frome* repainted in Southern Railway livery, newly delivered to Bricklayers Arms depot, 1925.
(F. Moore/John Scott-Morgan Collection)

A800 *River Cray*, lying on its side within hours of the accident at Sevenoaks, the damaged locomotive still in steam, 24 August 1927. (Waterman Album/Kent County Library)

Railway main line section between Woking and Walton-on-Thames where the 2-6-4Ts (and the 'King Arthur') rolled and rode roughly at around 60mph, so no tests were made at speeds of 75-80 mph which had been intended. A subsequent management meeting to discuss the results concluded that the Southern Railway's track was not good enough to accommodate regularly such heavy and speedy tank engines and the crucial decision was taken to rebuild them as 2-6-0 tender locomotives. This was before the inspector's final accident report which basically exonerated the locomotives, though it was

confirmed that they could roll when hitting weaknesses in the track at speeds of 50-60mph or above.

The prototype rebuilding involved A805 which was converted to become a 'U' nameless 2-6-0 between January and March 1928. It was matched with a 3,500 gallon tender and tested at speeds up to 75 mph between Ashford and Tonbridge without any rolling or lurching. The remaining members of the 'K' class were then converted to moguls between June and August 1928, although A800 was not back in traffic until December following repairs after its accident. A890 was converted retaining its

3-cylinder arrangement in June 1928 and became the prototype of the 'U1' class.

Operation

790 was run in between Ashford and Tonbridge on stopping trains and was allocated to Bricklayers Arms at the end of July 1917, from where it commenced trials on the important 1.30pm Cannon Street-Folkestone Junction express, a train weighing 340 tons. The schedule was maintained easily but there was concern about the adequacy of the water supply which was down to just 150 gallons at the end of the journey. The water consumption

was estimated at 26 gallons per mile, a not excessive amount, and it was decided that a stop for water at Tonbridge or Ashford would be necessary, so that the Folkestone non-stop services continued to be hauled by 4-4-0 tender engines. Its regular diagram consisted of the following:

3.40am Cannon Street – Folkestone (newspapers)
8.10am Folkestone – Cannon Street (Pullman)
4.18pm Cannon Street – Tonbridge (semi-fast)
7.36pm Tonbridge – Cannon Street (stopping train)

Both Folkestone services stopped at Tonbridge.

790 was transferred to Tonbridge depot in February 1922, at the time of a major timetable revision and then worked the following diagram:

8.07am Tonbridge – Cannon Street via Redhill
10.55am Charing Cross – Tonbridge via Redhill
12.42pm Tonbridge – Charing Cross via Sevenoaks
4pm Cannon Street – Tonbridge via Redhill

However, the track between Redhill and Tonbridge was substandard and after a broken rail in Penshurst tunnel was discovered without disastrous results, A790 was

removed from this diagram and returned to the Dover route working semi-fast trains.

After the building of A791-A799, and the springing modifications to A790 and test runs on Eastbourne expresses, A790-A794 were allocated to Brighton and A795-A799 to Eastbourne. The Brighton engines regularly worked the *Southern Belle* Pullman train and performed satisfactorily with loads of 320 tons. The test trains included comparative consecutive runs on the 11.05am Brighton-Victoria and the 3.05pm Victoria-Brighton (*Southern Belle*), using A792 for three days then LBSCR Baltic tank B331. The down load was normally 240 tons tare, although there was an

790 working a Tonbridge-Charing Cross train at an unidentified location, c1920.
(MLS Collection)

790 on a horsebox special for Epsom, with one coach at the rear for grooms, c1920.
(J.M. Bentley Collection)

A790, now named *River Avon,* at Croydon Windmill Bridge Junction with a train of ex LB&SCR six-wheel suburban coaches, c1925.
(John Scott-Morgan Collection)

extra coach on the first day, making the load 274 tons. The 2-6-4T performed consistently, beating the 60 minute schedule despite signal checks on two of the runs – and arriving over three minutes early on the unchecked journey. The Baltic tank just scraped in on schedule without any delays.

In the up direction, A792 had on average 216 tons against B331's 200 on two days and only 187 on the other. Despite this and an alleged small leak in its boiler, A792 outperformed the LB&SCR engine despite several heavy signal checks and a severe p-way slack. Holcroft was on the footplate on each run

with both locomotives and timed the trains to the nearest five seconds but did not record maxima or minima speeds. However, Cecil J. Allen published an excellent run he timed behind A799 on an Eastbourne express in a 1926 article in the *Railway Magazine* and it is shown in full below.

Victoria-Lewes, Autumn 1925
3.15pm Victoria-Eastbourne
A799 River Test
250 tons gross

Miles	Location	Times mins secs	Speed mph	Punctuality
0.0	Victoria	00.00		T
2.7	Clapham Junction	06.50		
4.9	Balham	09.55	37½	1 L
6.8	Streatham Common	12.20	52½	
9.4	Selhurst	15.55	46	
10.5	East Croydon	18.00	sigs to slow line	1 L
13.6	Purley	23.00	41	
15.0	Coulsdon	25.50	sigs to fast line	2¾ L
17.0	Star Lane Box	28.55	41½	
18.8	Quarry Box	31.15	42½	
21.9	Earlswood	34.15	70½	2¼ L
26.0	Horley	37.40	75	
29.6	Three Bridges	41.05	60	1 L
31.9	Balcombe Tunnel	43.45	53	
34.1	Balcombe	46.00	65	
38.0	Haywards Heath	49.25	74/ sigs 30*	½ L
41.2	Keymer Junction	52.55	30*	T
44.8	Plumpton	58.50	55½ /52½	
47.7	Cooksbridge	61.55	60	
50.2	Lewes	65.35	(62 minutes net)	½ L

In the summer of 1926 seven 'King Arthurs' with six-wheel tenders were allocated to the Central Section and as a result the five Brighton based 'Rivers' were moved to Eastbourne joining the five there. Their performance on the Eastbourne expresses was first class, but problems arose with their limited water capacity and during the autumn, with heavy trains, poor weather and need for steam heating, the water demand rose and after a number of instances when the 'River' had to stop for water (an ironic phrase in our climate) it was decided to move the 2-6-4Ts away from this route, with the various 4-4-0s including the LB&SCR B4Xs returning. A790 – 794 and A798 went to Redhill, A796 to Ashford and A797 to Reading.

By this time, the Brighton built 'K's were appearing and after running in on Brighton-Portsmouth services, seven of the new engines also went to Redhill and three to Reading. Both depots provided power for the Redhill-Guildford-Reading trains including the heavy

A793 *River Ouse* at Clapham Junction with a Victoria-Brighton express, c1926. (John Scott-Morgan Collection)

A795 *River Medway* passing Coulsdon with a Victoria-Sussex Coast train including two Pullman cars, 28 May 1927. (H.C. Casserley/J.M. Bentley Collection)

A804 *River Tamar* pauses at Clapham Junction with a Brighton-Victoria semi-fast service, c1926. (John Scott-Morgan Collection)

South Coast-Birkenhead through trains. However, with the transfer of the Eastbourne engines there also, A800-A804 were further transferred to Dover, working trains to Charing Cross and Cannon Street via both Tonbridge and Maidstone East.

The 3-cylinder A890 was initially rostered regularly to the 6pm Charing Cross-Dover Priory, where its acceleration (slightly superior to the 2-cylinder engines) was noted, although a spell of hard running could drain the boiler. Like the 'K's it was considered rough-riding and it is surprising that it was not called in for the springing modifications made to A790 and incorporated in the new build from A800. It derailed at 60 mph on the

Otford-Ashford line, near Wrotham, though once again the inquiry blamed the track rather than the engine. However, because of the poor state of the track on that route, all the 2-6-4Ts were banned from it. It was derailed again at Bearsted just a few days before the major derailment of A800 at Sevenoaks and, like the 'K's, was stopped until taken in for rebuilding in April 1928, having only run a total mileage of 48,983. Few records exist in detail of the performance of the 2-6-4Ts on the road – the only full log I have found being that of A799 quoted earlier and timed by Cecil J. Allen, although even that was only logged to the nearest five seconds, surprising for that gentleman.

Holcroft did ride on A890 several times (it was his 'baby') and he left some sketchy notes of runs made in early 1926. In April 1926, it was working the mid-morning train from Charing Cross to Dover, first stop Tonbridge, schedule 43 minutes with 287 tons. A late start gave the driver incentive to regain nearly three and a half minutes, most of them on the climb from New Cross to Knockholt. Three coaches were dropped at Tonbridge, and running was easy with the remaining load. Holcroft noted the engine was driven with full regulator and early cut-off. On the 6pm Cannon Street with 275 tons gross (a commuter train) there was a

A805 *River Camel*
on a London Bridge-
Sussex Coast express
in the South London
suburbs, c1927.
(R. Lissenden Collection)

problem at the start with shortage
of steam as the fire had not burned
through properly, but time was
kept despite this and after the
Tonbridge stop the boiler recovered
and all was well. The 26.7 miles
from Tonbridge to Ashford
were run in 29 minutes, though
unfortunately Holcroft gave us
no details of speeds. Holcroft
wrote in the second volume of his
autobiography:

'It was my last and most
memorable trip with No.A890

and as perfect as possible. The
shovelling plate on the bunker
and firehole door were on the
level, and so spaced that the
fireman could do his work by a
swing of the body without lifting
a foot. That, combined with the
beautiful smooth riding (sic),
resulted in the total absence of
spilled coal on the floor, and
the cab was dustless. Steam
pressure and water were well
up, and with the regulator fully
opened and cut-off close to mid-
gear the exhaust was inaudible.

The engine seemed to skim
along with the greatest of ease
under the restraint exercised;
the 26 ½ miles were reeled
off in 29 minutes start to stop
against a gently rising gradient.
It was a most pleasurable ride,
and my feelings of satisfaction
were enhanced by a proprietary
interest in the engine, since I had
been allowed a free hand in the
designing of those parts which
distinguished the three-cylinder
arrangement from that of the
two-cylinder.'

A801 *River Darenth* with an up Sussex Coast-Victoria express passing Coulsdon, c1927. (Real Photographs/J.M. Bentley Collection)

A802 *River Cuckmere* passing Deepdene (Dorking) at speed with a Kent Coast-Redhill-Reading train for the GWR interchange, 2 October 1926. (H.C. Casserley/J.M. Bentley Collection)

Chapter 4

THE 'U' 2-6-0S

Design & Construction

As a direct result of the Sevenoaks accident involving A800 *River Cray* and the inquiry findings and Board deliberations about the tendency of the 'River' tank engines to roll and ride roughly on parts of SR infrastructure, a decision was made at the end of 1927 to convert the 'K' 2-6-4 tanks to a tender 2-6-0 retaining frame, wheels, motion and boiler, but removing the water tanks and bunker and replacing the latter with a 6-wheel 3,500 gallon tender. A805 *River Camel* was the prototype and it entered Ashford Works in January 1928 and the rebuilding was complete by March. Test runs were immediately made between Ashford and Tonbridge to check the stability of the rebuilt locomotive, running at speeds up to 75mph without incident. Later trials from Hither Green encountered some unsteadiness between Sevenoaks and Tonbridge, not severe but causing the SR authorities to put a 70mph maximum speed restriction on the new moguls, which were classified as class 'U'.

As a result of the initial successful trials, conversion of the remaining 'K' tank engines was immediately commenced in February 1928, each rebuilding taking around three to four months.

The conversion dates, mileages completed in tank engine form before rebuilding and Works where the rebuilding took place were:

A790	6/28	313,973	Eastleigh
A791	7/28	63,730	Eastleigh
A792	7/28	69,994	Eastleigh
A793	6/28	64,040	Eastleigh
A794	6/28	63,185	Eastleigh
A795	6/28	52,478	Eastleigh
A796	7/28	52,405	Eastleigh
A797	7/28	49,534	Ashford
A798	8/28	47,975	Ashford
A799	7/28	60,932	Ashford
A800	12/28	40,128 (included major repairs following accident damage)	Ashford
A801	7/28	42,292	Ashford
A802	7/28	43,252	Ashford
A803	6/28	36,599	Brighton
A804	6/28	37,218	Brighton
A805	3/28	27,661	Ashford
A806	6/28	22,027	Brighton
A807	6/28	25,376	Brighton
A808	7/28	17,348	Brighton
A809	7/28	16,061	Brighton

Fourteen new tenders were constructed by Armstrong Whitworth and attached to A790-796, A802-804 and A806-809, and second-hand tenders of similar capacity from 'N' class locomotives were attached to A797-801 and A805. Despite their new classification, the 'U's were known to everyone as 'Rebuilt Rivers' or even just 'Rivers'.

The rebuilt engines weighed 63 tons, tender 40 tons 10cwt, giving a total engine weight of 103 tons 10cwt. Maximum axleload over the coupled wheels was 18 tons 16cwt. Other dimensions apart from the obvious length were the same as the 'K' tank engines.

In March 1926, before the critical Sevenoaks accident, the Southern Board, despite misgivings from the Running Department, had ordered twenty more 'K' 2-6-4Ts and allocated the numbers A610 to A629 to them together with the following names:

A610	*River Beaulieu*
A611	*River Blackwater*
A612	*River Bourne*
A613	*River Bray*
A614	*River Creedy*
A615	*River Ebble*
A616	*River Eden*
A617	*River Anton*
A618	*River Hamble*
A619	*River Wandle*
A620	*River Lymington*
A621	*River Medina*
A622	*River Meon*
A623	*River Okement* (changed from *River Exe*)

A792, formerly *River Arun,* at Victoria shortly after rebuilding, 1928. (MLS Collection)

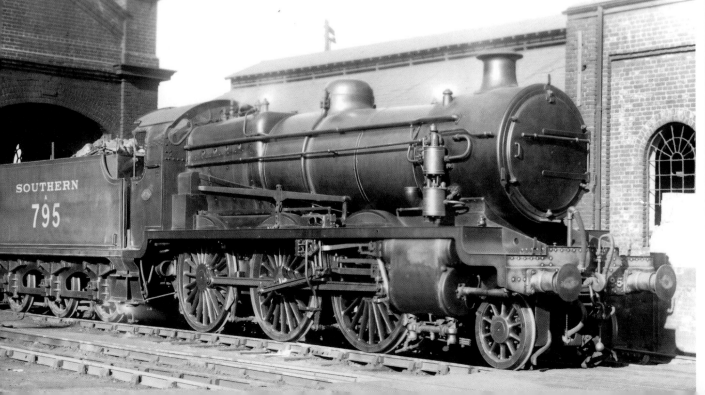

A795, formerly *River Medway,* at Bricklayers Arms, 1928. (Real Photographs/John Scott-Morgan Collection)

A624   *River Otter* (changed
        from *River Allen*)
A625   *River Parrett*
A626   *River Sid* (changed from
        River Tiddy)
A627   *River Tavy*
A628   *River Thames* (changed
        from *River Lymher*)
A629   *River Tichfield*

Fortunately, the tank engines had not been constructed before the decision was made to rebuild the 'K' tank engines as tender moguls, but Ashford Works had already cut twenty frames and cast all the cylinders. They were therefore constructed as 'U' class moguls from scratch in 1928 and 1929. A610-A619 were built at Brighton Works and A620-A629 were built at Ashford, but the proposed names were never

applied, although enthusiasts and railwaymen knew both the 16xx and 1790-1809 series of moguls as 'Rivers' in the 1930s. A further ten 'U's were ordered in March 1929 to be built at Ashford and these, A630-A639, which were never allocated names, were completed between February and May 1931. The A610-639 series varied slightly in outward appearance from the rebuilt 'K's by having slightly higher running plates, reducing the size of the splashers, two lookout windows instead of four and platform steps ahead of the cylinders. The engines were renumbered 1610-1639 and 1790-1809 in mid-1931.

A629 was built with German-designed equipment for burning pulverised fuel. A large enclosed hopper in the tender replaced the

coal area. The fuel was fed to the fire by two large delivery screws and an auxiliary one in the centre. The revised tender arrangement cut the water capacity to 3,300 gallons. The firebox was brick-lined and there were no firebars. Tests were conducted in the Ashford area until 1930 and it was later transferred to Eastbourne for comparative trials with A627. A629 proved unreliable, although it did manage some passenger services correctly. However, the amount of coal dust exhausted and deposited on the line (and adjoining gardens, not to mention hanging washing) caused severe complaints, and also caused a large number of lineside fires. A629 ran just under 3,500 miles in this form. Any savings in fuel costs were offset by

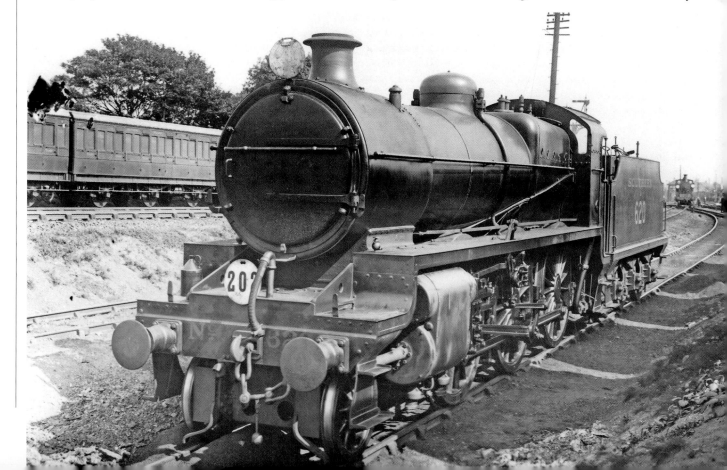

A620 at Salisbury, c1929. (F. Moore/ MLS Collection)

A611 at Clapham Junction, c1930.
(Photomatic/John Scott-Morgan Collection)

1626 after renumbering but before fitting with smoke deflectors, c1932.
(Colling Turner/MLS Collection)

compensation claims that had to be made to farmers for burnt crops. A629 (now numbered 1629) was returned to standard coal burning arrangement in October 1932.

The Central Division allocated engines were dual braked including Westinghouse air pumps, which were stripped from the engines transferred away from Battersea and Eastbourne when that route was electrified in 1933. In the mid-1930s, the moguls were fitted with smoke deflectors like many SR classes and in 1938-9 the flat-sided 3,500 gallon tenders of 1610-1629 were replaced by 4,000 gallon tenders with turned-in tops.

The locomotives had received standard Southern Railway lined green livery. 1624, 1625, 1635, 1806, 1807 and 1809 were painted unlined green at the start of the Second World War, but retained Maunsell lettering, but from January 1940 Bulleid lettering and cabside numerals became the norm. From April 1941 the green livery was replaced by wartime plain black.

After the war, the locomotives were rundown and there was a severe shortage of coal, so the Government pressed the railways to convert a substantial number of engines to oil-burning. The Southern Railway's allocation was 110 locomotives of which thirty were moguls, ten 'U's and twenty 'N's. Only two 'U's however had been converted before the Government (a different

A629 at Ashford during trials burning pulverised fuel, c1931. (John Scott-Morgan Collection)

1632 at Basingstoke, 25 April 1937. (MLS Collection)

1621 at New Cross shed, April 1937. (MLS Collection)

31632 still in wartime black, c1950.
(MLS Collection)

31804 at Ramsgate, 28 July 1953.
(MLS Collection)

Guildford's 31625
at Bricklayers Arms,
14 October 1956.
(MLS Collection)

31614 at Brighton,
14 September 1958.
(A.W. Martin/MLS Collection)

31801 at Eastleigh depot, 9 November 1958. (Colin Boocock)

Department!) discovered the country had insufficient foreign currency to pay for the oil. 1625 and 1797 had been converted at Ashford and 1629 's work had commenced but not been completed before the decision was reversed. 1625 and 1629 had their tenders replaced by 3,500 gallon straight-sided tenders to accommodate the oil-burning equipment (taken from 1803 and 1805 as the rebuilt 'Rivers' still had straight-sided tenders). Electric generators and batteries were fitted to provide headlamp illumination and cab interior lighting. 1625 and 1797 both worked around Exmouth Junction and Fratton where some of the other SR oil-burning engines were based. They had their oil-burning equipment removed in November 1948 having just run 27,903 (1625) and 33,169 (1797) miles in oil-burning mode. The other 'U's scheduled for oil-burning – 1613, 1616, 1635, 1637,

1638, 1795 and 1796 – were not affected in the end.

The entire class was renumbered 31610-31639 and 31790–31809 at nationalisation after initial use of the prefix 's' to a couple of moguls in the early months (s1620 and s1631). At first the 'U's were painted plain black, but from October 1948, commencing with 31628, the BR mixed traffic lined black livery was applied. It was 1955 before the last wartime black livery disappeared (31806).

In later years the frames gave problems as they were thinner than convention in order to reduce the weight (of the original 'K's) to the permitted axleloads of the early 1920s. Therefore, the frames of the 'U's (and also the 'N's) required heavy repair through patching and welding. Consideration was given to withdrawal of those engines with cracked frames in 1953, but since these engines were expected to be required until at least the mid-1970s,

31790, the rebuild of the 1917 'River' prototype, ex works at Tonbridge, 26 July 1959. (Colin Boocock)

31635 on the turntable at Redhill shed, July 1962. (Roy Hobbs /Online Transport Archive)

reframing of those worst affected was authorised. This was eventually restricted to the provision of new front ends with those engines being given new pattern cylinders, outside steam pipes and BR blast pipes at the same time. The locomotives improved in this way and the dates on which the modifications were made were:

Full frame renewal:	31615	6/60
	31621	2/55
	31625	1/59

	31628	1/57
	31634	4/55
	31637	10/59
	31791	1/61
	31809	9/60

Front end renewal:	31613	3/58
	31614	2/57
	31617	2/61
	31619	11/60
	31622	11/60
	31623	3/56
	31624	5/56
	31633	9/60

	31635	1/59
	31795	2/58
	31802	1/59
	31806	11/57

The strengthened frames caused a slight weight change, the axleload of the 31610-39 series being 18 tons 3cwt and the Rebuilt 'Rivers' 18 tons 14cwt. Most were fitted with AWS and spark arrestors. The conversions were entirely successful with the crews considering them an improvement on the engines that were not modified.

31619, c1962.
(Bill Gwyther/MLS Collection)

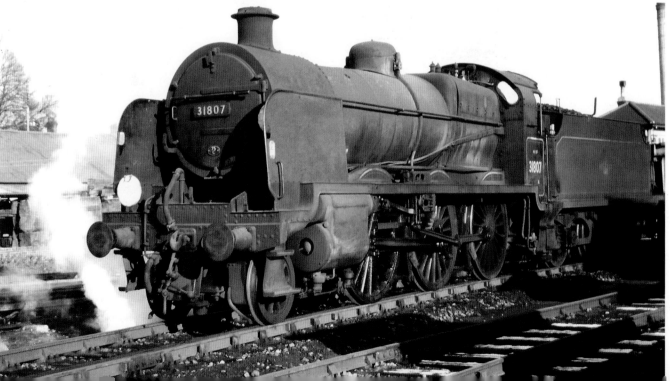

31807 at East Grinstead
Yard, in the winter
sunshine, 28 December
1963. (David Clark)

31799 at Guildford, c1964. (MLS Collection)

Because of earlier electrification than previously expected, Ashford Works closed in June 1962 and repair work of all the moguls was concentrated at Eastleigh. From that date, instructions were given that there should be no further major repair work to cylinders, frames or boilers and the first 'U' to be withdrawn in consequence was 31630 in November 1962.. It had run 897,941 miles. 31610 was withdrawn in December with 1.1million miles to its credit and eleven of the 31610 series and three 'Rebuilt Rivers' were withdrawn in 1963 (including two that had received major frame renewal as recently as 1960 (31615 and 31633). Ten remained at the end of 1964, all based at Guildford and were redundant when the Reading-Redhill line received DMUs in January 1965. However, a few goods and parcels turns on the South West main line remained with 31791, 31803, 31809 and 31639 lasting until 1966. The highest recorded mileage was achieved by 31794 at 1,155,902. The highest of the 1929-31 engines was 31618 at 1,143,942.

31795 rebuilt with new front end frame and BR pattern chimney at Southampton Central, 26 May 1958. (Colin Boocock)

31802 at Yeovil Town, the altered shape of the front end of the frame clearly visible. The front end of its frame was renewed in 1959 and it received new pattern cylinders at the same time, 16 June 1964. (MLS Collection)

31631 at Redhill shed, clearly showing the rebuilding with new front end frames, although this engine was not recorded as having had this change, autumn 1961.
(Roy Hobbs/Online Transport Archive)

31626 after withdrawal at Eastleigh, 2 May 1964.
(MLS Collection)

Operation

By the end of April 1929, the thirty-nine 'U's in service were allocated as follows:

Eastbourne:	A626 - A628, A790 – A799 (the 'Rebuilt Rivers' with Westinghouse brake)
Redhill:	A800, A804
Reading:	A801 - A803
Guildford:	A610 - A624
Nine Elms:	A625, A805 – A809

A629 was in Eastleigh Works undergoing conversion to burn pulverised fuel. The Eastbourne engines replaced ex LB&SCR B4X 4-4-0s on the London expresses and some Brighton-London services although the most important services on both routes were in the hands of the six-wheel tender 'King Arthurs'. The 'U's were well liked on the Eastbourne expresses and regularly exceeded their authorised maximum speed limit of 70mph. Nine Elms and Guildford engines worked the London-Portsmouth line and also services to Reading, Southampton via Alton, and Salisbury. They monopolised services on the heavily graded Reading-Redhill line running along the foot of the North Downs.

When the Brighton line was electrified in January 1933 all the Battersea and Eastbourne moguls were re-allocated as follows:

Yeovil:	1790-1795
Nine Elms:	1626, 1805-1809
Guildford:	1610-1625, 1627-1629, 1638, 1639, 1796-1799
Ashford:	1800, 1803
Dover:	1630-1635
Redhill:	1636, 1637, 1801, 1802, 1804

The newly allocated Yeovil engines replaced an equal number

One of the Eastbourne based 'Rebuilt Rivers' (A790 – A799) at the head of an Eastbourne-Victoria train composed of former LB&SCR vehicles, 1928.
(MLS Collection)

Dover based 1633 near Bromley on a South Coast-Midlands train via Kensington, c1932.
(John Scott-Morgan Collection)

Guildford's 1796 on a Nine Elms-Southampton Docks freight, c1932. (John Scott-Morgan Collection)

Redhill's 1802 on a Guildford-Redhill train at Betchworth, c1932. (John Scott-Morgan Collection)

Dover's 1635 on a freight on the Quarry line, Redhill, c1935.
(John Scott-Morgan Collection)

of 'T9' and 'S11' 4-4-0s on a variety of stopping passenger and van trains between Salisbury and Exeter. The Dover engines worked to Victoria via Chatham and the North Kent line. The two at Redhill worked the Margate-Birkenhead trains between Redhill and Reading.

S.A. Harvey timed a Dover engine, 1633, on a Tunbridge Wells-London Bridge train on 25 February 1933. 'E4' 2514 worked the 2-coach train to Tonbridge where the load was made up to 180 tons and 1633 took over. The 14.1 miles to the Godstone stop

were covered in 18 minutes, three less than schedule with steady running at 58 mph. Nutfield was also reached early, but the train was stopped outside Redhill for nearly two minutes and was 2½ minutes late in. Three vehicles were detached there and 1633 proceeded with only 90 tons, stopping at Purley, East Croydon, Norwood Junction and arriving at London Bridge two minutes early. Maximum speed was the upper 50s, sustained from Penge to New Cross Gate.

In May 1935, 1627-1629 were transferred to Bournemouth and

were utilised on the Poole-Brighton trains and on cross-country services to Newcastle as far as Banbury. Basingstoke later got an allocation for working Waterloo-Salisbury semi-fasts and Basingstoke-Portsmouth/Southampton trains. In the summer Basingstoke borrowed 'U's from Nine Elms and Guildford for services running to the West Midlands via the GWR at Reading. One also acted as a standby engine at Basingstoke in case of a failure on the main line. After a failure on one occasion of the locomotive working the down *Bournemouth Belle*, a 'U' set off in a hurry and the crew ignored the 70mph restriction. Eastleigh had been asked to provide a relief locomotive, but the 'U' was going so well that the crew were happy to take the mogul through to Bournemouth West although a Bournemouth 'King Arthur' was supplied for the return working.

In 1936, the Waterloo to Portsmouth direct line was not yet electrified – it would be the following year. The Rev. R.S. Haines travelled frequently between Petersfield, Havant, Fratton and Portsmouth Town in the mid-1930s and kept copious notes of every journey. Former LB&SCR engines were often on his trains between Portsmouth and Havant, going along the coast to Eastbourne and Brighton – mainly 'B4X' 4-4-0s and 'I3' 4-4-2Ts. From Portsmouth to Petersfield he travelled behind 'Schools', 'King Arthurs', Urie 'N15' and H15's, Drummond D15's and the odd 'L12', 'S11', 'T9' or even 'L11'. Most frequent of all, however, especially on the stopping trains which the reverend gentleman used most often (was he visiting his parishioners or truanting to train spot?) were the moguls. In his complete survey of June and July 1936 which I have analysed in detail, he had 38 runs behind 'U' moguls in the 16xx series, 19 runs behind 'Rebuilt Rivers' and six behind 'U1's. He annotated each line of entry classifying the engine performance as exceptional, very good, good, poor or very poor. If no comment, it was considered ordinary or 'average'. Of the 38 16xx 'U' runs, one was exceptional, five

very good, eight good, four poor and two very poor. 18 had no comment. Of the 19 'Rebuilt Rivers' runs (he called all the 'U's, of both series, 'Rivers' which apparently was their universal nickname in the 1930s), four were exceptional, four were very good, three were good, eight were 'average' and none were poor or very poor. He seemed

to have a good opinion of the 1790-1809 series. He commented several times particularly about the excellence of 1799, one of the Guildford engines.

In the summer of 1936 (June-September) he recorded 534 runs behind 203 different engines of 24 different classes. On the semi-fast and stopping services he used most frequently he had:

98	D15	15	U1	3	S11
69	V (Schools)	12	N15 (Urie 'Arthur')	1	T3 (Adams)
62	U	11	H15 (Urie)	1	A12 (Adams)
56	I3	9	N15X ('Remembrance')		
53	L12	8	N15 ('Scotch Arthur')		
37	B4X	6	K10		
30	T9	4	Lord Nelson		
22	S15 (Urie)	3	T1 (Adams)		
18	T14	3	M7		

Additionally, he commented that he had four GW locomotives (Churchward 2-6-0s) and twenty-one miscellaneous LB&SCR tank engines on the short hop between Havant and Fratton/Portsmouth. I conclude that the Rev. Haines must have been retired and spent the summer travelling to and fro several times a day between Petersfield and Portsmouth. All ten of the 'Schools' allocated to Fratton were in evidence. The 'Lord Nelsons' were running in from Eastleigh. At this time the 'Schools' were on the fastest trains, and the semi-fasts on which Rev. Haines mostly travelled were the domain of the 'D15's and the 'U's and 'U1's.

Summer Saturday traffic conditions saw the moguls out in force with Nine Elms using one on the 1.22pm relief Waterloo-Swanage and the Lymington Pier

trains. West of Bournemouth speeds in excess of 80mph were recorded with 'U's in the Wool area. Rev. R.S. Haines timed a morning semi-fast Basingstoke-Waterloo from Woking on 28 May 1938, with 1633 pulling ten lightweight coaches, about 320 tons gross. It passed Weybridge in 7 minutes 16 seconds at about 60mph and just touched 70mph before Esher, passing Hampton Court Junction in 11 minutes 57 seconds and then easing to arrive at Waterloo after a signal check outside in 30 minutes 3 seconds (29 minutes net).

During the Second World War, Basingstoke, Reading and Nine Elms gained numbers for main line freight working, especially to Southampton Docks. Six Guildford 'U's went to Exmouth Junction in exchange for smaller wheeled 'N's for freight services from the Docks

1617 pilots a Fratton 'Schools' 933 *Kings Canterbury* on a Portsmouth-Waterloo express, c1935. (John Scott-Morgan Collection)

1806 at Waterloo with a Waterloo-Portsmouth train. M7 0-4-4T No.33 is engaged in Waterloo-Clapham Junction ECS duties, c1936. (John Scott-Morgan Collection)

1806 stands at Waterloo ready to depart with a Portsmouth train, c1936. (John Scott-Morgan Collection)

to Reading and the Midlands. Very high mileages between repairs were countenanced during the war, the average being nearly 94,000, with 1792 of Yeovil amassing 106,809. At the end of the war four went to Dover and were used on the many military specials that ran to bring troops and service materials home from the continent.

After the war, the allocation reassembled as follows:

Reading:	1610, 1611, 1620, 1627, 1628
Dover:	1631, 1639, 1807, 1808
Nine Elms:	1613, 1616, 1617, 1619, 1637
Guildford:	1798, 1799, 1800 – 1806, 1809
Basingstoke:	1614, 1615, 1621-1625, 1629, 1632-1634
Salisbury:	1612, 1618, 1626, 1630, 1636
Fratton:	1796, 1797
Yeovil:	1790-1794
Exmouth Jcn:	1635, 1638, 1795

All the 'U's and 'Rebuilt 'K's were still working at nationalisation and in 1950 31624 was equipped with tablet exchange and tested on the Somerset & Dorset line between Bournemouth and Bath Green Park. However, this does not seem to have been successful and 31624 returned to base. The 'U's did however share with GW engines (usually Churchward moguls) the running over the former M&SWJR from Andover to Cheltenham, there were two diagrams every day. Drummond 'D15' 4-4-0s continued to be the regular power

1614 on an excursion for the Southampton line, near Hook, c1938. (John Scott-Morgan Collection)

1615 stands at Redhill station with the through Margate-Birkenhead train which it will work as far as Reading General station, c1938. The train is formed on alternate days with SR and GWR stock. (John Scott-Morgan Collection)

1624 at Codford with a Portsmouth-Bristol train, 5 July 1938. (H.C. Casserley/ John Scott-Morgan Collection)

Basingstoke's 1625 on a freight near Aldershot at the junction for the Tongham branch, c1947. (John Scott-Morgan Collection)

1631, reallocated to Salisbury from Dover, heads a Yeovil Junction-Salisbury stopping train still using LSWR carriage stock, near Wilton, c1947. (MLS Collection)

Basingstoke's 1614 on a Waterloo-Salisbury semi-fast train near Hook, c1946. (John Scott-Morgan Collection)

for the Lymington Pier boat trains (restricted length because of the Brockenhurst turntable), but occasionally a 'U' would deputise, until 'Schools' displaced from dieselisation of the Hastings route took over.

A Guildford 'U', 31625, was timed on a 9 coach (325 ton gross) train on the 6.12pm Dover Priory-Charing Cross as far as Sevenoaks on 17 April 1954, but it seemed to struggle and after leaving Westenhanger and attaining 55mph at Smeeth, left Ashford 1½ minutes late. It made no more than 54½ mph before Headcorn, fell to 48 at Marden ,

touched 55 at Paddock Wood and was 3½ minutes late into Tonbridge. The climb through Hildenborough to the Weald Box was painful, falling

to 22 mph and arrival at Sevenoaks was nearly six minutes late. Poor steaming was suspected.

In mid-1955 the allocation was:

Nine Elms:	31617, 31621, 31634
Guildford:	31616, 31622, 31624, 31625, 31627, 31628, 31730, 31631, 31797-31800
Reading:	31612
Redhill:	31611, 31614, 31615
Eastleigh:	31613, 31618-31620, 31629, 31801-31804 (3 sub-shedded at Andover for the Cheltenham services)
Bournemouth:	31632
Salisbury:	31635, 31636, 31639
Yeovil:	31610, 31623, 31626, 31790-31796
Fratton:	31637, 31638, 31805, 31807-31809
Basingstoke:	31806

31809 preparing to depart from Bournemouth Central with the 11am to Sheffield, 27 August 1955. (Colin Boocock)

31624 at Eastleigh with a Reading-Southampton Terminus train, 14 June 1956. (Colin Boocock)

31620 leaving Cheltenham Lansdown for Andover and Southampton, c1956. (MLS Collection)

31620 Leaving Cheltenham Landsdown for Andover and Southampton, C.1956. (MLS Collection)

31623, with rebuilt front end and cylinders, at Southampton Central with a train for Bristol composed of mainly WR coaching stock, 15 June 1957. (MLS Collection)

31791 leaving
Southampton Central
with a Portsmouth-
Cardiff train in the late
1950s. (Colin Boocock)

31802 stands in
the middle road at
Bournemouth Central
ready to work a stopping
train to Southampton
and Basingstoke,
10 February 1957.
(Colin Boocock)

31614 on a down goods at New Milton in the New Forest, 6 April 1956. (MLS Collection)

31807 at Broadstone with a train of former LSWR stock, 4 August 1956. (MLS Collection)

The Yeovil engines were again working the most mileage between general repairs. They were kept in excellent condition, with regular turns to Exeter and Portsmouth and at weekends through working to the North Devon coast on excursions. After 1959, they worked to Weymouth including banking duties at Evershot and northbound from Weymouth. 31632 had a regular turn west of Bournemouth with goods and local passenger turns to Dorchester. Bournemouth's two 'Lord Nelsons' (30864 and 30865) were regularly outstabled at Dorchester for a starting turn, but if problems occurred 31632 deputised as far as Bournemouth Central. I have traced a log showing a typical working at this time, with 31631 of Guildford on the 6.40pm Bournemouth West-Basingstoke, with just three coaches and a van. It was early into Southampton Central and left on time. It stopped at St Denys and Southampton Airport very promptly, was early into Eastleigh but left there five minutes late. With 47 at Shawford, it picked up a couple of minutes to Winchester and was doing 47 at Wallers Ash and 50 mph at Micheldever and arrived at Basingstoke exactly on time. Basingstoke's lone 'U', 31806, was timed on a light (3-coach 105 tons) Reading-Eastleigh/Portsmouth train on 14 April 1961, and although stopping at Reading West, Mortimer, Bramley, Basingstoke, Micheldever and Winchester, was quite lively between stops touching 57 mph before Mortimer, 64 before Micheldever and 66 at Winchester Junction.

A very good effort was timed on this section behind the same 'Rebuilt River', 31806, on 19 May 1961. It had 10 vehicles 298 tons tare, 320 tons gross

and the train was the 5.50pm Portsmouth-Reading, which was recorded between Eastleigh and Basingstoke. I give details below:

Eastleigh-Basingstoke, 19 May 1961
31806, Basingstoke
10 chs 298/320 tons

Miles	Location	Times mins secs	Speed mph	Schedule
0.0	Eastleigh	00.00		4¾ L
0.85	Allbrook Box	02.33	20/42	
3.85	Shawford	07.43	51	
6.95	Winchester	12.58		4¾ L
0.0		00.00		6¼ L
2.1	Winchester Jcn	04.32	51	
4.8	Wallers Ash	08.11	44/55	
8.5	Micheldever	13.19		2½ L
0.0		00.00		2 L
1.85	Roundwood Box	04.32	24/61	
5.55	Wootton Box	08.18	59/66	
7.8	Worting Junction	10.41	57/68	
10.3	Basingstoke	13.50		¾ L

In 1960, Yeovil's whole allocation was exchanged with engines from Guildford and Eastleigh to concentrate engines with spark arrestors there to avoid complaints from farmers re lineside fires. However, the crews removed them when they found the equipment impeded steaming. In 1963, all sheds west of Salisbury were transferred to Western Region control, including the 'U's at Yeovil which were replaced by WR based Standard '4' 4-6-0s during 1963-4. Also in 1963 a number of 'U's returned to the Central Division at Bricklayers Arms for mainly goods work in Surrey and the Tunbridge Wells

area following the withdrawal of all the 3-cylinder 'N1's by the end of 1962. The Redhill-Reading route continued to be the main area for their use until the end of steam there in January 1965.

The workload for the remaining 'U's in 1965-6 was much reduced involving a few Basingstoke-Waterloo semi-fasts and van services and parcels train working around Reading/Clapham Junction at Christmas 1965. In 1966, the last survivors were in demand for 'farewell' railtours, involving 31639 and a surviving 'N'. 31791 also participated in special working and both were finally withdrawn in June 1966.

31612 at Basingstoke with a semi-fast train for Waterloo, c1962. (MLS Collection)

31613, with new front end to the frames, on a down goods at Sway, 13 June 1962. (MLS Collection)

31622 at Winchester City with a train of LMR rolling stock from Cheltenham Lansdown to Southampton via Andover, 1 September 1962. (David Clark)

31627 at Swaythling with a freight, 31 May 1961. (MLS Collection)

31637, a mogul that has had complete renewal of frame and cylinders, at Semley with a Salisbury-Exeter stopping train, c1959. (J. Davenport/MLS Collection)

31791, another mogul with complete frame and cylinder rebuilding, between Woking and Brookwood on a Waterloo-Salisbury semi-fast train, c1961. (MLS Collection)

31632 on an Exeter-Salisbury stopping train nearing its destination, passing Quidhampton near Wilton, 27 August 1963. (Rodney Lissenden)

31793 arriving at Salisbury with a local train from Basingstoke, 27 August 1963. (Rodney Lissenden)

31790, the prototype rebuilt 1917 'River', at Deepcut near Woking on a Woking-Eastleigh p-way train, 5 September 1964. (Rodney Lissenden)

31639 leaves Lyndhurst Road with the 4.10pm Southampton Terminus-Bournemouth, 6 October 1965. (David Clark)

31807 with an up train at Sandling Junction, 27 May 1961. (David Clark)

31631, recently ex-works, departs Chilworth with a Reading-Redhill stopping train, September 1961. (Ken Wightman)

31807 at Crowthorne with the Birkenhead-Ramsgate ('Conti') inter-regional express formed of Southern Region stock, August 1962. (Ken Wightman)

31790, the rebuild of the 1917 prototype 'River', at Farnborough North with a Reading-Redhill train, 20 July 1963. (MLS Collection)

31619 at Guildford station with the 9.45am Reading-Tonbridge, 2 September 1964. (MLS Collection)

31791 leaving Betchworth with the 12.40pm Redhill-Guildford, 4 October 1964. 31791 had new frame replacement in April 1960. (David Clark)

A clutch of surviving moguls on Redhill shed – 'Rebuilt Rivers' 31803 and 31791 and 'N' 31405, October 1964. (Roy Hobbs/ Online Transport Archive)

Six moguls, 'U's and 'N's, on Redhill shed, May 1964. (Roy Hobbs/ Online Transport Archive)

'Rebuilt River' 31803 and the last surviving 'N' 31411 at Mayfield en route to 'Haywards' Heath with the RCTS *Wealden* railtour, 13 June 1965. (Roy Hobbs/Online Transport Archive)

31639 and 'N' 31411 doublehead an LCGB railtour, just before final withdrawal, 3 April 1966. (Roy Hobbs/Online Transport Archive)

The last surviving 'U' moguls, 31791 and 31639, on an RCTS special 'farewell' tour at Windsor & Eton station, 30 April 1966. Both locomotives were withdrawn in June. (David Clark)

Preservation

31618

31618, built at Brighton in 1928, was withdrawn from Redhill depot in January 1964 and was sold to Woodham Brothers, Barry, and was stored there pending scrapping until 1968 when it was resold to the Southern Mogul Preservation Society for £2,000. It moved to New Hythe in 1969 and was refurbished externally until transferred to the Kent & East Sussex Railway in 1972. Its potential use was very limited there because of weight restrictions and in May 1977 it moved to the Bluebell Railway at Sheffield Park where it was restored for active operation. It is attached to a 3,500 gallon straight-sided tender. It last worked in 1994 when it was withdrawn pending the required 10-year overhaul. It is currently on static display, painted in the BR mixed traffic lined black livery.

31625

31625 was built at Ashford in March 1929, and had a full frame renewal in January 1959. It was withdrawn from Guildford shed in January 1964 and was sold to Woodham Brothers in Barry. It was restored and is owned by John Bunch and is on long term hire to the Swanage Railway where it is currently being overhauled with a view to returning to traffic shortly.

31638

1638 was built in 1931 at Ashford. It arrived on the Bluebell Railway in 1980 and, after restoration, was returned to service for the first time in 42 years in February 2006. The boiler ticket expired in January 2016, but due to a number of minor faults and the need for a new hydraulic test, it was decided to withdraw it from service in July 2015. 1638 has been a reliable performer over the last nine and a half years, although requiring a couple of spells in the works for boiler and firebox repairs, and has borne the brunt of the heavier services on the Bluebell over its period in service. It is currently painted in SR green livery,

31625 rebuilt with new frame and cylinders, at Eastleigh Works, 15 April 1959. (Colin Boocock)

numbered 1638 and is on static display awaiting overhaul.

31806

A806 was built at Brighton in 1926 as a 'K' ('River') class 2-6-4T, named *River Torridge.* Following the Sevenoaks accident involving A800 in 1927, it was rebuilt as a 2-6-0 in 1928 and withdrawn in January 1964 and sold to Woodham Brothers at Barry in 1966. It was eventually rescued eight years later in 1974 and moved to the Mid Hants Railway for restoration. Owned by John Bunch, it was hired on a long term contract by the Swanage Railway in 2014 and is currently operational

there with its boiler ticket not due for renewal until 2021.

Personal Reminiscences of the 'U's

My first memory of a Southern mogul is very hazy. Somewhere around 1947 or '48, when I was about nine, I spent a day with my great aunt and uncle in Guildford. Uncle George had been an engine driver at Guildford until his retirement through ill health in 1929 (he eventually lived to 98) and as a treat he took me down to the shed and put me on the footplate of the shed pilot (30458 *Ironside*) as we dragged a

dead 'U' out of the depths onto the turntable to place it on a different road for repair.

The moguls next came into prominence in my life when I moved schools from Surbiton to Charterhouse. The Waterloo-Portsmouth Harbour line through nearby Godalming was steam-free, apart from the daily pick-up freight which was usually hauled by a Maunsell mogul based at Guildford. The nearest steam action was on the Redhill-Guildford-Reading line, known colloquially as 'the Rattler'. I would frequently cycle the five miles from the school over the Hogs Back to the railway line just west

Preserved 31806 on the Watercress Line at Medstead & Four Marks about to power the 5.33pm train to Alresford, 24 September 1983. (MLS Collection)

The pick-up goods from Fratton and Petersfield to Woking passes through Godalming behind 'Rebuilt River' 31800, 21 June 1955. (David Maidment)

Another photo of the pick-up goods from Fratton and Petersfield to Woking approaches Peasmarsh Junction, Guildford, behind 'Rebuilt River' 31800, 23 June 1955. (David Maidment)

31637 departs from Guildford station with a Redhill-Reading train, March 1959. (David Maidment)

of Wanborough station, the first after Guildford towards Reading. There were still the occasional former SE&CR 'D' class 4-4-0s to be seen, but the line was dominated by the Maunsell 'U's with the odd 'N' thrown in. In my trainspotting days, I virtually completed copping all the 'U's, in particular the 316xx series, many of which were shedded locally at Guildford. My folding Kodak 'Brownie' camera with its limited 1/25 shutter speed could not cope with the train speeds crossing the bridge where I watched, but on a wet Sunday in 1955 I cycled to Shalford on the other side of Guildford and tried to take a few photos as trains arrived or departed at the station there. As well as the Maunsell engines, by that time Redhill Standard '4' 2-6-0s had displaced the Wainwright D's, so my bag was 50/50. I also found a spot near Ash Junction where I attempted some shots. In March

1959, after leaving school and moving to Woking, I spent a few days with the camera recreating my school experience taking shots west of Woking itself, but also finding my old haunts around Ash Junction.

The Charterhouse Railway Society carried out a survey of operations on the Weybridge-Basingstoke main line on a peak summer Saturday in 1956 (28 July). Every movement between 1pm and 7pm was documented. Surprisingly the number of 'King Arthurs' in action (Urie and Maunsell) outnumbered the Bulleid pacifics, but I, based at Woking, recorded the movements of five 'U's. Two were working empty coaching stock – 31621 and 31625 – but a 'Rebuilt River', 31799, appeared on an afternoon semi-fast from Andover (due Waterloo at 2.34pm) and two were operating the Lymington Pier boat trains, 31624 on the Waterloo

2.46pm arrival and 31634 due at 4.04pm. The 'U's were the stop-gap on these trains between the Drummond 'D15' 4-4-0s and the arrival of the 'Schools' to take over these services completely in 1958. There were three up Lymington Pier boat trains that day, and something must have gone awry with the mogul booked for the third as it tore past Woking with

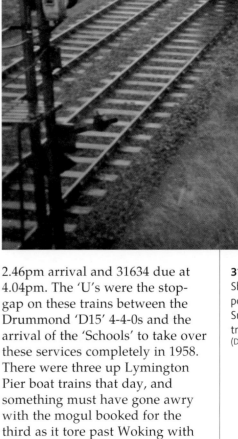

31631 rushes into Shalford station in the pouring rain with a Sunday Redhill-Reading train, 19 June 1955. (David Maidment)

There was one 'U' in the opposite direction, though the BR Standard '4' moguls were dominant eastbound returning to their own depot at Redhill. Here 31635 enters the cutting near Ash Junction, March 1959. (David Maidment)

One afternoon by the lineside produced 'U' after 'U' on westbound Redhill-Reading trains – first 31616, then 31617, followed by a 'Rebuilt River', 31800, March 1959. (David Maidment)

Urie 'N15' 30747 *Elaine*. This engine could not be turned on the short turntable at Brockenhurst so it must either have run light tender first from Eastleigh if the mogul had failed there, or replaced a failed engine at Eastleigh on the up run.

Between November 1957 and June 1960, I travelled on weekdays to University College near Warren Street in London and had an annual season ticket (price £33). Although I amassed a vast mileage behind Bulleid pacifics, 'Lord Nelsons', 'King Arthurs', 'Schools' and Standard 4-6-0s, the moguls did not get a look-in until the Maunsell 4-6-0 classes were substantially reduced in numbers through withdrawals. Then, on summer Saturdays, the occasional 'U' would appear on the Basingstoke or Salisbury semi-fasts instead of 'H15s' or 'L1s' which had turned out in previous years as the 4-6-0s tackled longer distance holiday reliefs. I continued travelling to London when I joined British Railways in a clerical post in August 1960, and in that August, I timed a couple of runs on successive Saturdays with 'U's, both of which ran very energetically, although their loads were moderate:

Waterloo-Woking and return, August 1960
12.42pm (SO) Waterloo-Basingstoke
31634 Nine Elms
6 chs/205 tons
13 August 1960

Miles	Location	Times mins secs	Speed mph	Punctuality
0.0	Waterloo	00.00		T
1.6	Vauxhall	02.53		
3.15	Queens Road	-	58	
4.0	Clapham Junction	06.12	40*	
5.65	Earlsfield	08.55	pws 22*	
7.3	Wimbledon	12.55	sigs 10*	
9.85	New Malden	16.12	60	
12.15	Surbiton	18.37	66	
13.45	Hampton Court Jcn	-	sigs 5*	
14.5	Esher	22.01	42	
15.95	Hersham	-	56	
17.2	Walton-on-Thames	25.32	60	
19.2	Weybridge	27.46	61	
	West Weybridge	-	71	
21.75	West Byfleet	30.41	sigs 25*	
24.4	Woking	34.51	(27 net)	3¾ L

2.34pm Waterloo arrival from Andover,
31628 Guildford
6 chs, 200 tons
6 August 1960

Miles	Location	Times mins secs	Speed mph	Punctuality
0.0	Woking	00.00	(slow line)	T
2.65	West Byfleet	04.02	67	
5.2	Weybridge	06.26	64	
7.2	Walton-on-Thames	08.24	71	
8.35	Hersham	-	73	
9.9	Esher	10.48	sig 20*	
10.95	Hampton Court Jcn	-	15* to ML	
12.25	Surbiton	14.11	46	
14.55	New Malden	16.58	58	
17.1	Wimbledon	19.51	60	
18.75	Earlsfield	22.35	pws 15*	
20.4	Clapham Junction	25.10	47*	
21.55	Queen's Road	-	54	
23.0	Vauxhall	28.28	sigs 0*	
24.4	Waterloo	32.58	(27½ net)	2 L

I joined the Railway Enthusiasts' Club in 1959 and their club room was adjacent to Farnborough station on the South West main line. On many a summer Saturday during 1959, 1960 and 1961, I would catch a lunchtime semi-fast from Woking (usually a 'Scotch Arthur' or 'S15'), and then return in the late evening on the last stopper from Eastleigh which sometimes had a Urie S15, but more often was a 'U' or later, an Eastleigh Standard '4' mogul. In my travels around Guildford seeking photo spots and the journeys back from Farnborough, I was hauled by the following moguls over those relatively short stretches: 31610, 31612, 31615 (2 runs), 31618 (2), 31622 (3), 31623, 31624, 31625 (2), 31627 (3), 31628, 31630 (4), 31631 (3), 31632 (2), 31633, 31634, 31635 (4), 31636 (2), 31637, 31639, 31792 (3), 31793, 31797 (2), 31798 (4), 31799, 31801, 31806 (2), 31807 (2) and 31809, ie 53 separate runs, but little more than 500 miles of haulage in total.

After September 1961, my career took me full time to the Western Region and my return to my Woking family home was spasmodic with few opportunities to travel behind the dwindling Maunsell classes. In 1963 and '64 I was in South Wales and in the summer of 1964, when I was stationmaster at Aberbeeg in the Western Valley above Newport, I travelled home on my weekend off on the Saturday morning from Newport on a couple of occasions on the 9.10am Llanelli (09.55am Swansea) to Brockenhurst via Westbury and Dorchester. Motive power was a Llanelli 'Grange' to Westbury, a BR Standard '5'

31809 passing Pokesdown with the 9.55am SO Swansea-Brockenhurst holiday train, 20 July 1963. The author took this train on a couple of Saturdays the following summer, although both times it was hauled by a Bulleid pacific between Dorchester and Brockenhurst. However, the train was banked at Evershot by 'U' 31802 on both occasions. (G.M. Shoults/MLS Collection)

4-6-0 to Dorchester and a Bulleid pacific to Brockenhurst. The point of interest here is that on both occasions the train was banked by a 'Rebuilt River', Yeovil's 31802, up the four miles from Yetminster to Evershot summit, mainly 1 in 51.

Chapter 5
THE 'U1' 2-6-0S

Design & Construction

Following a couple of derailments of 3-cylinder 2-6-4T A890 *River Frome* and the disastrous accident that befell A800 on defective track near Sevenoaks in August 1927, a decision was made to rebuild the tank engines as 2-6-0s, and the 2-cylinder engines became class 'U' as outlined in the previous chapter. The decision affected A890 also. Although it had shown itself

to be the better of the tank engines in the tests on the LNER East Coast main line, the Southern Railway Board did not have the confidence in the state of their own railway's track to allow these locomotives to continue to run without rebuilding as tender engines. A890 followed some of the 'K's into Ashford Works and it emerged in June 1928, retaining its conjugated valve gear and three cylinders and was classified 'U1'. It also lost its name.

It closely resembled the 3-cylinder 'N1', the main difference being the larger coupled wheel diameter and in outward appearance, the splashers over them. It was provided with a 3,500 gallon tender that had been attached earlier to an 'N'.

The authorities ordered ten further 3-cylinder 2-6-0s in March 1928, a demonstration of confidence in the basic design as no rebuilt 'Rivers' had yet been tested.

A890 *River Frome* at Tonbridge, 17 July 1926. (H.C. Casserley/J.M. Bentley Collection)

The newly rebuilt 'K1' 2-6-4T as the prototype 3-cylinder mogul, the forerunner of the new 'U1' class, June 1928. (MLS Collection)

The first two, numbered A891 and A892, emerged from Eastleigh Works in January 1931, with a few changes to A890. The most important difference was the replacement of the conjugated valve gear with three sets of Walschaerts valve gear. They also had straight running plates from the deep front buffer beam, rather than a raised plate over the cylinders, smaller splashers, front footsteps and tenders with turned-in tops to 4,000 gallon tenders. Dimensions

otherwise were similar to 'K1' A890, and weighed 65 tons 6cwt, with the tender 107 tons, 14cwt. A893-A900 followed between February and May, and the building continued as the Southern Board had ordered twenty more 'U's or 'U1's in March 1929. In fact, a further ten 'U1's were built, numbered 1901-1910 (the SR renumbering occurred at the same time as the building of the first of the second batch, 1901, in June 1931). The last, 1910, was completed in November that year.

When A890 was brought into the Works for its first major overhaul after rebuilding in December 1931, its conjugated valve gear was replaced by a set of Walschaerts gear to the inside cylinder in line with 1891-1910, and it returned to traffic in February 1932 as 1890.

The 'U1's were fitted with smoke deflectors in the mid-1930s along with most SR passenger classes – in fact the three-cylinder moguls had been particularly problematic with drifting smoke obscuring the

The brand new 3-cylinder 'U1' 895 at Waterloo on a train for Portsmouth, March 1931. (John Scott-Morgan Collection)

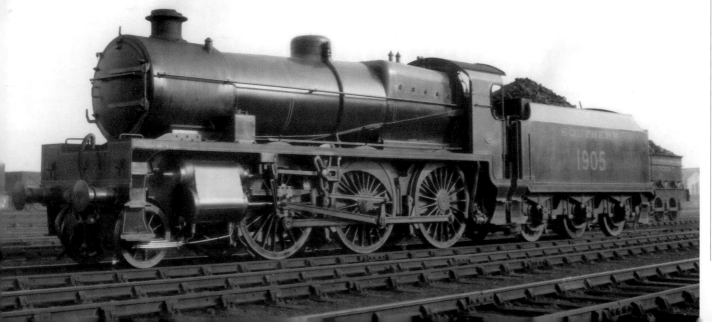

1905, one of the second batch of U1's ordered in March 1929 and delivered in the summer of 1931, seen here at Eastbourne, August 1931. (Colling Turner/ MLS Collection)

The penultimate 'U1', 1909, built in October 1931, shortly after delivery and being put into traffic, 1932. (John Scott-Morgan Collection)

1895, one of the first ten 'U1's, after the fitting of smoke deflectors, c1934. (J.H.L. Adams/MLS Collection)

The last of the first order of U1's completed in May 1928, after the fitting of smoke deflectors and during their trials in the West Country, on the turntable at Plymouth Friary, c1938. (John Scott-Morgan Collection)

1902 at Brighton, c1949. (MLS Collection)

driver's view, as their exhaust blast was softer than that of the two-cylinder engines.

Like most SR engines, the 'U1's worked high mileages during the Second World War and were in need of Works attention when hostilities ceased. Their Southern Railway lined green livery had been replaced by plain black during the war and this continued for a while at nationalisation, with 1891 and 1901 acquiring the prefix 's', before the others of the class received the full renumbering as BR 31890-31910. Finally, the BR lined black mixed traffic lining was applied from November 1948, starting

with 31905. 1908 retained its SR number and plain black livery until December 1953 and 31891 was the last to be repainted in lined black in May 1954.

In the mid-1950s it was found necessary to build new cylinders for the 'U1's (and 'N1's), most being outsourced to private companies for their manufacture. However, unlike the two-cylinder engines, their frames did not suffer fractures and so it was unnecessary to replace the frames, even partially. In BR times, they were fitted with AWS and BR type blast pipes similar to the Standard '4' 4-6-0s and 2-6-0s.

After the Kent Coast electrification in 1959, it became harder to justify extensive repairs. The last engine to receive a general Works repair was 31903 in November 1960. At the end of the 1962 summer timetable, most were stored and the first to be condemned were 31897, 31902 and 31904 in November 1962. Thirteen 'U1's were withdrawn en masse at the end of the year and all had gone by July 1963, the last survivor being 31910. The penultimate withdrawal in June 1963 was the rebuild of A890 itself, 31890, which had run 1,026,340 miles in its life. No other 'U1' achieved a million miles, the nearest being 31895 at 934,916.

31890, the rebuilt 2-6-0 from A890 *River Frome* with its unique 'U1' raised running plate over the outside cylinders, at Bricklayers Arms, 4 April 1959. (Colin Boocock)

31907 at Stewarts Lane, 31 May 1958. (Colin Boocock)

31898 stopped for repair at Tonbridge shed, 23 May 1959. (MLS Collection)

31895 in final BR mixed traffic livery at Redhill on a down parcels train, December 1962. (Roy Hobbs/Online Transport Archive)

31895 in final BR mixed traffic livery after withdrawal and stored in Eastleigh Yard awaiting scrapping, condemned in December 1962 after running 934,916 miles, 8 June 1963. (MLS Collection)

Operation

The 'K1' had run just 49,000 miles in its original form. After its conversion to 2-6-0, A890 began its new life operating out of Bricklayers Arms, being tested initially on the Hastings line, then from Waterloo to both Weymouth and Portsmouth, but its 70mph maximum speed limit and its weakness on the banks compared with the 'L' 4-4-0s that were operating the Hastings route services meant that its stay on that line was shortlived and

it was reallocated to Battersea to work on the Kent Coast services via Chatham. The flange wear on the numerous curves on the Hastings route was also a problem with the three-cylinder engines; the same problem existed when they were tried west of Exeter later. However, it had been more successful on the Portsmouth direct services from Waterloo and the production engines A891-A900 were all allocated to Fratton to replace the Drummond D15's that had been the mainstay of

operations on that route. They apparently performed well on this route, but in 1934 after electrification of the Brighton line and with further building of the 'Schools', they were replaced at Fratton by ten new engines of the latter class.

1900 (from Fratton) and 1901, 1902 and 1904 were initially allocated to Eastbourne where they replaced the 2-cylinder 'Rebuilt Rivers', but in November 1931 Nos.1900-1910 were all at Eastbourne, where they stayed until

1891 shortly after construction at Waterloo with a Portsmouth train, 1931. (Real Photographs/ MLS Collection)

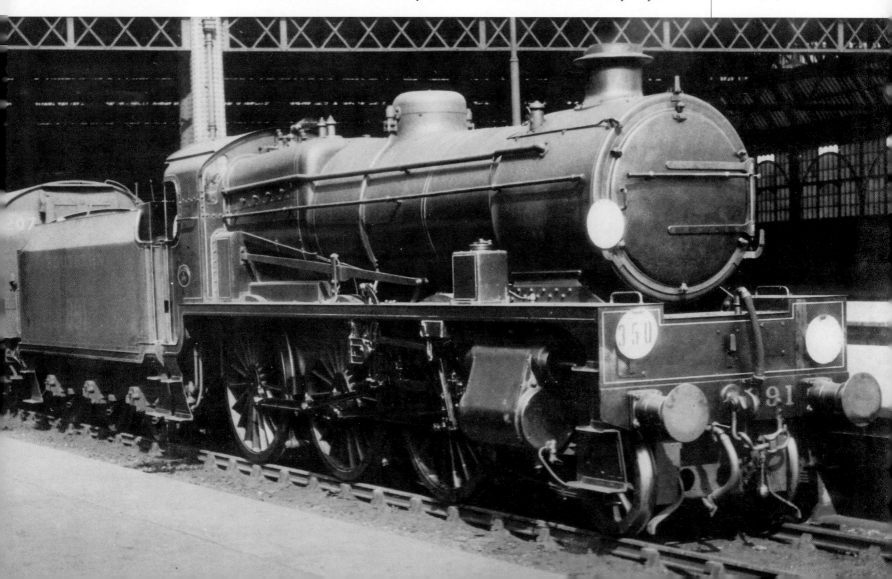

1902 on a Dover-Victoria train, 1931. (F. Moore/ MLS Collection)

Eastbourne's 1902 at Hampden Park Eastbourne with a local train, 1932. (John Scott-Morgan Collection)

the electrification of the Brighton line in 1933. However, eleven 'U1's returned to Eastbourne in 1934 replacing the LBSCR Baltic tanks and a few 'Schools' until further electrification in 1935 made them redundant there.

On trial the 3-cylinder moguls had been lighter on fuel than the 2-cylinder 'U's, but in practice in regular operation the 'U1's gained the reputation of being heavy on firemen, particularly on the Western Section. Comparative coal consumption figures of the 'U's at Yeovil and the 'U1's at Fratton in 1933 showed an average of 36.7lb coal burned per mile for the 'U's compared with 39.2lb for the 'U1's, but this may have been because of the difference in work required from those routes. It has been suggested that the three cylinders drained the boiler quickly when the 'U1's were working hard causing firemen to overfire as a precaution, but without comparison over the same route it is difficult to draw any clear-cut conclusions.

Finding detailed logs of 'U1's has not been easy, especially of their time at Fratton when they were the line's main express power. The only full log I have discovered before the advent of the 'Schools' to take over the key trains is one by J.M. Robbins of a run from Petersfield to

An Eastbourne based 'U1' in the 1900-1909 series, on a Victoria-Eastbourne train in the Coulsdon area, just before electrification was inaugurated, 1933. (J.M. Bentley/John Scott-Morgan Collection)

Waterloo on 25 February 1933 with 1894, although I have to admit that it was a pretty mediocre performance. The train was the 6.15pm from Petersfield to Waterloo, allowed 79 minutes for the 55 miles, including a four minute scheduled stop at Guildford. The load was 8 coaches, including a dining car, 262/270 tons and the train left Petersfield 9¼ minutes late on a stormy night with heavy rain. 1894, one of the ten Fratton 'U1's, accelerated to 49mph down the mile or so of 1 in 115 before the ten mile climb to Haslemere summit began. It fell from that speed to 28mph on the two miles of 1 in 80 after Liss, had recovered to 37mph on the easier grades to Liphook, then held 40mph on the final two miles on the 1 in 100 to Haslemere which was more respectable. The tempting four miles descent to Witley and two miles 1 in 82 to Milford produced nothing over 50mph which suggests that the regulator was closed as the fireman recouped the boiler pressure. 55mph round the restricted curves of Godalming was the maximum before the Guildford stop. The time for the 24½ miles was 36 minutes 45 seconds, with just one slight signal check to 25mph at Shalford Junction on the final approach to Guildford. Just one minute had been recovered and the train arrived 8 minutes late and left just 5 minutes late after smart station work. Performance fell away after that. There was a dead stand before Woking Junction for 40 seconds, that town being passed 12 minutes late at 27mph. 60mph in the dip past Brooklands trailed away to

55mph at Weybridge and with speed hovering between 55 and 59 mph, Hampton Court Junction was passed 12½ minutes late. 51mph at New Malden, 56 at Wimbledon and a final fling at 61 down the 1 in 338 before Clapham Junction passed 13½ minutes late, was met by the final indignity of a dead stand for 1½ minutes as a freight got the path ahead crossing out of Nine Elms depot. Arrival at Waterloo was 17 minutes late.

The only other evidence of their work on the Portsmouth line that I can find comes from the 1936 records of the Rev. R.S. Haines, accessed via the Railway Performance Society archive. This is a massive record – some 25 pages scanned from his notebook giving sketchy details of some 500 runs in that year between Petersfield, Havant and Portsmouth. Of the 182 different engines noted on these trains, 15 were U1's – 1893 (4 runs), 1894, 1895, 1898, 1899 (3), 1900 (3) and 1902 (2). I've traced the runs of seven of these during the summer of 1936, which Rev. Haines classified: 1 excellent; 2 very good; 3 good and 1 poor. All the runs were between Petersfield and Havant or return – I suspect the clergyman lived at Havant as many other runs are just from Havant to Fratton or Portsmouth. I give below some of the data he recorded.

Petersfield-Havant, Summer 1936

		1899 5 chs 26 June		1893 4 chs 4 July		1893 4 chs 16 July		1895 10 chs 29 May	1899 6 chs 18 Sept
0.0	Petersfield (1:100 R)	00.00	21L	00.00	4L	00.00	T	00.00	00.00
2.4	Buriton Signal Box (1:80 F)	04.55		05.18		04.26		05.31	05.19
8.4	Rowlands Castle (1:120 F)	12.38 00.00		13.23 00.00		12.21 00.00		12.28 |	15.12 00.00
11.5	Havant	05.38		06.47		05.27		17.33	05.09
Rev. Haines assessment		**Good**		**Good**		**Very good**		**Excellent**	**Poor**

Havant-Petersfield

		1893 5 chs 4 July	1893 3 chs 18 July
0.0	Havant	00.00	00.00
3.1	Rowlands Castle (1:120 R)	06.16	05.50
9.1	Buriton Signal Box (1:80 F)	10.03	22.32 * sig stand (freight train ahead)
11.5	Petersfield	13.14	25.41
		Good	**Good**

On being displaced at Fratton 1892-1896 were reallocated to Nine Elms where they worked freights and some semi-fast passenger trains to Salisbury and Portsmouth. Others went to Battersea but 1894 and 1895 stayed on the Western Section at Feltham and 1898 at Basingstoke.

Then four of the Eastbourne engines went to Guildford for the Reading-Redhill services, as well as being augmented power for the Portsmouth slow and semi-fast trains, as identified by Rev. R.S. Haines. As early as the winter timetable of 1935 some 'U1's were unemployed and

stored until 1937 when 1900 had an extended trial in the West Country on 'T9' duties. It was obviously more than competent to do this comparatively light work, though whether it was at reduced cost is problematical. Nevertheless 1900 was joined by more,

The rebuilt A890 *River Frome*, now the prototype 'U1', passing Bromley with a Ramsgate train, 1 June 1936. (H.C. Casserley/John Scott-Morgan Collection)

so that the class allocation at the commencement of the summer 1937 timetable was:

Nine Elms:	1890 – 1892
Battersea:	1896, 1897, 1901 – 1910
Exmouth Junction:	1893 – 1895, 1898 – 1900.

Later that year the Nine Elms engines were transferred to Exmouth Junction, also 1896 and 1897 from Battersea, whilst 1900 returned to Battersea, thus dividing the class almost equally between the two depots.

The three cylinder configuration and the smoother running with short-cut-offs and full regulator meant that drivers were often tempted to exceed the 70mph limit that had been set for the moguls. S.A.W. Harvey recorded a number of journeys between Bromley South and Chatham in the late 1930s on which he logged some speeds well in excess of that officially permitted:

Bromley South-Chatham, c1938
1.03pm Bromley South (12.35pm Victoria-Ramsgate)

		1897 304/325 t			1901 320/345 t			1907 340/360 t		
Miles	Location	Times	Speed		Times	Speed		Times	Speed	
0.0	Bromley South	00.00			00.00			00.00		
1.7	Bickley Junction	05.03			05.25			06.00	sigs	
3.9	St Mary Cray	07.42			08.12			08.55		
6.8	Swanley Junction	10.48		¼ E	11.28	sigs	½ L	12.00		1L
9.6	Farningham Road	13.28	74		15.55	70		14.35	76	
12.5	Fawkham	16.05			19.20			17.00		
15.0	Meopham	19.08			23.05			19.40		
16.0	Sole Street	20.23	47	¾ E	24.25	46	3½ L	20.43	56	¼ E
20.0	Cuxton Road	24.58	50		28.10	80		24.15	76	
22.0	Rochester Road Bridge	27.40		1¾ E	30.55		1½ L	27.07		2½ E
22.8	Rochester	28.50			32.12			28.30	sigs	
23.4	Chatham	30.23		1½ E	33.20 (31 ½ net)		1¼ L	30.22 (28¾ net)		1½ E

1891 on a Dover-Victoria train near Bromley, c1938. (MLS Collection)

Rochester-Bromley South, 1939

		1909 225/245 t		
Miles	Location	Times	Speed	Punctuality
0.0	Rochester	00.00		T
0.8	Rochester Road Bridge	02.20		
2.8	Cuxton Road	06.45		
6.8	Sole Street	14.42	31	¾ L
7.8	Meopham	16.10	60	
10.3	Fawkham	18.45		
13.2	Farningham Road	21.07	80	
16.0	Swanley Junction	24.45	pws	¾ L
18.9	St Mary Cray	28.40		
21.1	Bickley Junction	31.35	sigs	½ L
22.8	Bromley South	34.45		¾ L

The start of the Second World War disrupted this pattern as the power of the 'U1's was needed for increased freight traffic, especially over the Reading-Redhill route to the channel ports, while "T9's returned to their erstwhile duties in the West Country which they could perform with comparative ease.

The 'U1's were, not surprisingly, biased to freight operations during the war and ran substantial mileages between repairs. They also worked troop trains and were the regular steeds for the heavy daily Ashford-Newcastle train from Redhill to Banbury via Reading and Oxford before handing over to LNER power.

Mr A.J. Baker timed a number of these inter-company through trains between Redhill and Guildford, where engine performance needed to be of a high level, as the loads were substantial and the trains stopped in the dip at Deepdene in both directions preventing a run at the banks. Deepdene was a safer administrative headquarters for the Southern Railway during the war.

Redhill-Guildford, 1942
Ashford-Newcastle through train

| | | 1895 | | 1890 | | 1890 | |
| | | 11 chs 362/380 t | | 12 chs 388/410 t | | 12 chs 395/415 t | |
Miles	Location	Times	Speed	Times	Speed	Times	Speed
0.0	Redhill	00.00		00.00		00.0	
1.8	Reigate	06.13	24/21	05.34	25/20	05.51	25/22
4.6	Betchworth	10.05	53/44/57	09.34	54/44/57	10.27	55/sigs 20*
7.2	Deepdene	13.32	pws 20*	13.08	pws 20*	14.24	pws 20*
0.0		00.00		00.00		00.00	
0.7	Dorking North	02.44	28/24	02.52	24 ½/20½	02.36	28/22½
5.4	Gomshall	12.58	60/51	14.20	55/43	13.08	54/42
9.4	Chilworth	18.20	sigs	19.01	57	18.03	54½
11.2	Shalford	20.52	sigs	21.24		20.27	
11.9	Shalford Junction	22.13		22.33	30*/sigs	21.25	40*
13.1	Guildford	25.28	2 E	26.20	1½ E	23.46	4½ E

Guildford-Redhill, 1942
Newcastle-Ashford through train

| | | 1895 | | 1890 | |
| | | 12 chs 371/395 t | | 13 chs 414/435 t | |
Miles	Location	Times	Speed	Times	Speed
0.0	Guildford	00.00		00.00	
1.2	Shalford Junction	03.38	35*	03.34	35*
1.9	Shalford	04.52	40/28	07.48	40/29
3.7	Chilworth	07.56	31/21	07.48	31/21½
7.7	Gomshall	16.37	45/31	16.23	45/31
12.4	Dorking Town	23.10	58	22.33	62
13.1	Deepdene	24.22	5½ E	23.37	6½ E
		00.00		00,00	
2.6	Betchworth	07.22	25/23	07.35	25/23
5.4	Reigate	12.03	44/31	12.31	46/sigs
7.2	Redhill	18.11	sig stop 2¼ L	17.03	1 L
		(24½ + 15¼ net)		(23½ + 15¾ net)	

After the war they powered relief boat trains on the reopened Newhaven-Dieppe continental route, and also boat trains via the Chatham route to Dover. By this time the Southern was being flooded with the new Bulleid light pacifics so further repercussions occurred, with U1's 1980-1894 replacing 'N's on the Victoria-Uckfield trains until the Brighton built 2-6-4Ts in turn replaced them.

The authorities seem to have been at a loss to know what to do with these relatively modern three-cylinder moguls, so they were next tried on the Waterloo-Lymington Pier trains, with 31907-31910 working these from Nine Elms in the summer of 1952. O.S. Nock had a footplate trip on 6 August from Waterloo to Brockenhurst and back

at this time with Nine Elms' 31907. The down trip was heavily loaded with Isle of Wight holidaymakers, so the train weighted 370 tons gross, and with five booked station stops, six signal checks including two dead stands, it lost 11½ minutes on the running time, just about schedule net of delays. With steam pressure hovering around 160-170lb psi, speed did not reach 60mph until West Weybridge. After the Woking stop, acceleration was slow to 43mph at MP 31 and again speed was only in the 50s until 60 was reached just before Basingstoke, where pressure had risen to 190lb psi. The run downhill to the Winchester stop was livelier with 72½ just before the slowing and 66 before the Eastleigh scheduled halt, but pressure fell to 145lb

after Southampton and the engine struggled to reach 50mph through the New Forest.

The return journey with 365 tons was much better and punctual, the fireman had got used to the engine and a loss of one minute running time was made up by smart station working. The 'U1' had run 75,000 miles since its last heavy overhaul, but was in reasonable condition and touched 70-72 mph without too much discomfort. However, the fireman had not worked on a 'U1' before and tended to overfire causing some steaming anxieties in the early stages. At the end of the summer they were once again relegated to freight and parcels train work to Guildford or Reading and the following summer the Drummond 'D15' 4-4-0s got the

1906, still in Southern Railway wartime black and SR numbering and lettering, climbing Sole Street bank with the 3pm Ramsgate-Victoria, eighteen months after nationalisation, 6 June 1949. (Ken Wightman)

31905, now repainted in BR mixed traffic lined black, at Shortlands Junction with a van train from Ramsgate, 1951. (Ken Wightman)

An unidentified 'U1' leaves Bromley South with a summer relief for the Kent Coast, 1952. (Ken Wightman)

Lymington Pier boat train tasks which they kept for several years. By 1954 the four 'U1's were back on the Eastern Division, at Stewarts Lane, Tonbridge and Bricklayers Arms.

31906 was then tried on the Somerset & Dorset with 'U' 31621 and coped adequately with eight coach loads, but lost time when trials included loads up to twelve vehicles. The Western Region imposed a 45mph speed limit on them on the line north of Evercreech Junction, and they were replaced there successfully by new BR Standard '5's. In view of the general lack of focus for these engines, it is difficult to understand how BR justified new cylinders for the class, though they stopped short of renewing frames which was necessary for several of the 'U's. They were by now concentrated on the Eastern Division and included the Hastings route amongst their duties, playing second fiddle to the 'Schools' along with 'L's, 'L1's and 'N's. A regular traveller

analysed 109 runs on the steep climb from Tonbridge to Tunbridge Wells, initially 1 in 47, then varying between 1 in 72 to 1 in 300 to High Brooms. Fifteen of the runs were with 'U1's where they were slightly better than the 'L's and 'L1's, but inferior to the 'N' and 'N1's and well short of the 'Schools' performance. When comparing the best runs of each class, the U1's came last.

In November 1954 the allocation of members of the class was:

Bricklayers Arms:	31890, 31891, 31896, 31897
Hither Green:	31892, 31893
Redhill:	31894, 31895, 31898, 31899
Brighton:	31900-31903
Stewarts Lane:	31904-31907
Tonbridge:	31908-31910

For a short while the Brighton engines deputised when necessary for Bulleid pacifics on Brighton-Bournemouth and Salisbury trains,

but they were back on the Eastern Division by the summer of 1955, working relief expresses to the Kent Coast as holiday traffic by rail built up in the 1950s. This reached its peak in 1957 when on one July Saturday no fewer than eleven of the class were noted on Kent Coast expresses. This lasted until the electrification of the Chatham line in 1959 when they were once again dispersed, with Tonbridge shed having as many as ten (31901-31910) while two went back to Brighton for inter-regional trains to Willesden, two to Feltham for freight work and three to Stewarts Lane for Central Division activities.

With the completion of further Eastern Division electrification in 1961 they now found themselves displaced by BR Standard '4' 2-6-4Ts for the remaining steam services in the Tonbridge area, and the final distribution of the class before inroads through withdrawals were made was:

Brighton:	31890, 31891
Three Bridges:	31892-31894
Feltham:	31895-31897
Salisbury:	31898, 31899
Exmouth:	31901-31904
Junction:	31901-31904
Nine Elms:	31905-31910

Their work on the Western Division was almost entirely on freight allowing the venerable Drummond class '700' 0-6-0s to be withdrawn. A few returned in the last few months to Stewarts Lane and Brighton shortly before withdrawal, but most had been withdrawn by the end of 1962 with the four at Brighton, 31890, 31891, 31901 and 31910, just lasting into the first half of 1963.

Prototype 'U1' 31890 at Shortlands on a Ramsgate-Victoria express, summer 1954. (Ken Wightman)

31895 on a Victoria-
Ramsgate express at
Bickley, 4 August 1955.
(MLS Collection)

Brighton's 31903 at
Bournemouth Central
with a train for Brighton,
12 March 1955.
(Colin Boocock)

A busy time at Eridge with 'U1' 31896 and a BR Standard '4' 2-6-4T waiting in the platform, 21 April 1956. (R.C. Riley)

31905 at Downs Bridge, Shortlands, with a relief Victoria-Ramsgate express, August 1958. (Ken Wightman)

The rebuilt 'K1', 31890, at Whitstable with a Victoria-Ramsgate express, 18 August 1958. (N. Harrop/MLS Collection)

31909 at Portsmouth & Southsea with a train for Eastleigh, c1960. (MLS Collection)

31891 leaving Redhill Tunnel with a South Coast – Midlands holiday express formed of Western Region rolling stock, 22 July 1961. (Roy Hobbs/Online Transport Archive)

31903 at Eastleigh with a Woking-Southampton Terminus train, 21 June 1961. (MLS Collection)

31907 leaves Winchfield with a Waterloo-Basingstoke semi-fast train, 7 August 1961. (David Clark)

31908 climbs Dorking bank with the 10.18am Redhill-Reading, 22 September 1962. (David Clark)

31901 at Crowborough on the 7.55am Brighton-Tonbridge just before withdrawal, 10 June 1963. (David Clark)

The oldest, 31890 (ex 'K1' *River Frome*) was withdrawn in June 1963 and 31910 was the last survivor being condemned just a month later.

Personal Reminiscences of the 'U1's

Apart from the odd sighting if one had ventured onto the South Western main line after attention at Eastleigh Works, most of my meetings with engines of this class were their occasional meanderings onto the Redhill-Reading line during the 1950s when I was at nearby Charterhouse and in the March 1959 period when I was taking short rail trips out of Guildford to take photographs in the Shalford area on the Redhill side or Wanborough and Ash on the west. I had short hauls behind 31903-31905 and 31908. However, I ran in to them unexpectedly in 1959 when I made

31894, a 3-cylinder 'U1', an unusual interloper, on a Reading – Redhill train, descends round the curve from the Reading line into Guildford station, March 1959. (David Maidment)

a number of sorties to Victoria to sample runs out to Bromley South before the imminent electrification of the North Kent line via Chatham. I was keen to get runs behind the six-wheeled tender 'King Arthurs' assuming they would be withdrawn after the June electrification date, not expecting the transfer of most of them to Nine Elms, Salisbury and Eastleigh. I also tried for runs behind the Maunsell rebuilds of the Wainwright 4-4-0s – the 'D1's and 'E1's.

I discovered that both the 1.35pm and 2.35pm Ramsgate trains from Victoria were candidates for 'King Arthur' haulage and got 30800 and 30806, and 30805 and a 'D1' (31505) on the return from those trips. Encouraged, I had the opportunity in May 1959 to try again despite the fact that perhaps I should have been revising for my impending finals exams. Somewhat to my initial disappointment, but that overcome when I realised the novelty, I found 'U1' 31891 at the head of the 1.35pm Victoria and duly travelled out to Bromley – I can remember little of the journey and did not time it, so I can now safely assume that it was not a disaster nor was it scintillating enough to be memorable. A week later, I tried the 2.35pm and got sister engine 31894. To add to my disappointment at the time, I got

Standard '5' 4-6-0s in the Stewarts Lane 73080-73089 series back on both occasions – at a time when the Nine Elms 73110-73119 were all too common on my journeys to and from Woking. Looking back on it,

however, I'm glad that I had the variety of at least a couple of runs with 'U1's on expresses, even if the distance was relatively short and the route gave little opportunity for speed.

31891 at the head of the 1.35pm Victoria to Ramsgate which the author took as far as Bromley South, May 1959. (David Maidment)

Chapter 6

THE 'W' 2-6-4TS

Design & Construction

The Southern Railway's programme of electrification had a few snags that few realised. With the increase in frequency and speed of services, especially in the morning and evening rush hours, the passage of freight trains through the system without undue delay to either the commuter or goods services became difficult. With third rail electrification rather than overhead, goods yards and sidings could not be electrified for staff safety reasons, so steam hauled freight services had to intrude into the electrified areas. Whilst the 'N' and 3-cylinder 'N1' classes had the power and acceleration to be the most appropriate power for such freight traffic, they were tender engines and less suitable for short distance freight, especially in the congested London area, where the need for turntable access would import further delay.

Maunsell therefore saw that a tank engine version of the 'N' would be most appropriate, especially for cross-London and other freights in the suburban areas. He had experience of the 'K' 2-6-4T and its 3-cylinder version, the 'K1', and was by the late 1920s only too aware of their reputation for rough-riding and rolling, but the system needed a slower speed freight version. A 3-cylinder engine would give faster and steadier acceleration of heavy freights on the heavily graded routes round London with their many sharp curves, junctions and flyovers and so the Ashford Drawing Office prepared a design of a freight smaller wheel version of the 'K1' and Maunsell got the acceptance of the Southern Railway Locomotive Committee to build ten 2-6-4Ts with 5ft 6in coupled wheels at a cost of £9,210 each – a rapid inflation of costs after the financial crash of 1929-30. In fact, because of the Depression, freight traffic receded drastically for a while, so the order was suspended until mid-1931, when the Running Department indicated that the engines were then required.

Five 2-6-4T locomotives, 1911-1915, were constructed in the first two months of 1932, with 5ft 6in coupled wheels, three 16½in x 28in cylinders, weighing a solid 90 tons 14cwt, axleload 19 tons 5cwt, with good adhesion and braking capabilities. There were some materials left over from the conversion of the passenger 'K's to moguls, especially the water tanks, bunkers and bogies and these parts were reused in the construction of the 'W's as these engines were classified. The cabs had side windows and the bogie wheels were fitted with brakes as braking power was essential on heavy freights moving in congested areas. They were built at Eastleigh and, after running in, were despatched to Stewarts Lane for freight work in the London area. They were painted black with single green lining.

There was the intention to build the remaining five locomotives of the authorised order in 1932, but the return of freight traffic after the recession was slower than anticipated, and the construction of these was again postponed, as was the subsequent 1930 order of a further five engines. Finally, in 1935, traffic had built up sufficiently to warrant construction of the outstanding orders and Ashford constructed 1916-1925 between April 1935 and April 1936, costs having fallen to £8,944 per machine. The construction work was transferred from Eastleigh to Ashford as Eastleigh was heavily committed in the building of the 'Schools' class 4-4-0s.

All were running in routine freight work for the remainder of the pre-war period, the only variation being the adoption of the Bulleid livery lettering and numerals from 1939. During the war period, with many of the

1913 at Bricklayers Arms, c1932. (F. Moore/John Scott-Morgan Collection)

1912 at Battersea (Stewarts Lane) c1935. (John Scott-Morgan Collection)

1917 at an unidentified location, c1935.
(John Scott-Morgan Collection)

1919 at an unidentified location, c1936.
(John Scott-Morgan Collection)

1923 at Hither Green
shed, 3 June 1939.
(MLS Collection)

moguls engaged in troop train and other war related activities, the 'W's found themselves frequently rostered to longer distance freight traffic. Despite their continued use in London, no serious war damage was sustained by any of them.

After nationalisation, these locomotives were renumbered 31911-31925 and continued in plain black freight livery. There was a brief flirtation with the idea of running them on some passenger services, but after running trials at speed, any plan was aborted.

General Heavy and Intermediate repairs were carried out usually at Ashford Works, although a few went to Brighton. 31916 was repaired at Eastleigh in 1948, but this was unusual. There were no spare 'W' boilers, though 'N' class boilers could be used if necessary.

Type 3 1,550hp diesel locomotives became available for freight work on the Southern Region from 1960 and in 1961 an overall speed restriction of 45mph was imposed on the class, though removed on the Oxted branch later. After dieselisation

of freight work on the Southern Region's Eastern and Central Divisions, a few went to Exeter for banking duties and were transferred to Western Region stock when the line west of Salisbury was subject to Regional boundary change in July 1963. The 'W's were either condemned by the WR or returned to the SR London area and all were gone by the end of the 1964 summer timetable. None was preserved. The highest mileage run by any of the class was just under half a million miles by 1932-built 31912.

1915, still awaiting BR numbering and lettering at Stewarts Lane, 22 May 1948. (MLS Collection)

31912 at Hither Green, 9 May 1959. (R.C. Riley)

31914 at Stewarts Lane shed, 10 May 1959.
(R.C. Riley)

31925 at Hither Green shed, 21 February 1960.
(R.C. Riley)

31918 at Bricklayers Arms depot, 28 October 1961. (Colin Boocock)

31922 and 'Z' 30952 at Eastleigh, 16 June 1962 . (MLS Collection)

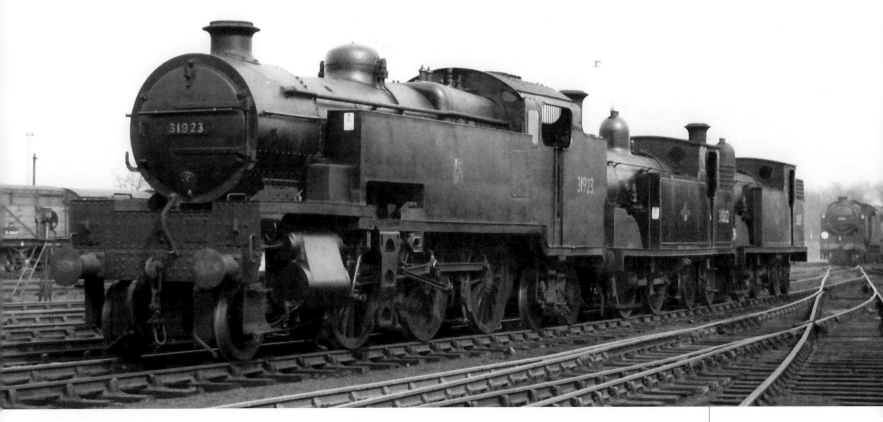

Operation

After construction at Eastleigh, the first five locomotives were run in on local freight work emanating from the Eastleigh area. One, 1915, went to Bricklayers Arms and worked various goods turns from Hither Green Yard to Kent destinations, whilst the others immediately were put to work on cross-London freights to Feltham, Acton, Willesden, Brent and Ferme Park, where they were well received.

The 1935 new arrivals operated in the Hither Green-Norwood Junction area, and allocated to the newly opened Norwood Junction depot. 1920-1925 were sent to Hither Green. By mid-1936, the allocation was:

Battersea (Stewarts Lane):	1911-1913
Norwood Junction:	1914-1920
Hither Green:	1921-1925

The work was almost entirely on cross-London freight work, although members of the class could occasionally be found outside their normal sphere of influence on weekend engineering or electrification trains. Slight readjustments were made in the allocation and in 1939, Battersea had gained two (1914 and 1915) at the expense of Norwood Junction. The wartime period did not change their duties significantly although freight frequency and loads increased substantially. All fifteen locomotives worked

high mileages between repairs, 1922 clocking up over 102,000 miles in a year and a half. In the preparations for D-Day, the 'W's had to supplement the 'N' diagrams as those engines were required for much of the military traffic. Those 'W's not required for London area freight working were outstabled at Chislehurst goods yard in steam during the severe London bombing raids. They were mostly unscathed, although 1919 was derailed by falling masonry at Balham in February 1941 and 1916 was attacked and hit by aircraft cannon fire when running over the Redhill-Tonbridge line en route to Ashford Works in January 1943.

After the war, the fifteen locomotives continued on their

31923 at Feltham with a couple of 'M7' 0-4-4Ts and another 'W' and a 'Q1' in the background, 25 March 1962.
(David Clark)

cross-London freight work. By 1948 the allocation was:

Battersea (Stewarts Lane):	31912, 31914, 31915
Norwood Junction:	31911, 31913, 31921-31925
Hither Green:	31916-31920

Because their riding was said to be fairly rough, there was some surprise when 31918 was subjected in 1948 to a series of trials on passenger trains on the Central Section from Victoria to Oxted and Tunbridge Wells with a view to replacing the ageing 'I3' 4-4-2Ts. The trials to test the riding at speed were conducted between Ashford and Tonbridge where a couple of tests with empty six-coach sets almost achieved even time runs over the 26 miles with speeds in excess of 70mph, although allegedly the riding was extremely rough. Apparently, the riding when running bunker-first was much improved, but the trials were

considered unsuccessful and the 'I3's continued on the Oxted line until Brighton built LMS Fairburn 2-6-4Ts were introduced (see chapter 9).

The Hither Green 'W's were frequently used on Sunday engineering trains on the Eastern Division during 1948-50. A couple experienced minor accidents with the derailment of 31913 on a sharp curve at High Brooms Shell Oil depot in 1949 and 31919 crashed into the stop blocks of a catch-siding at Clapham Junction after the driver misread signals in 1960.

With the introduction of the Crompton Class '33' diesels in 1960 some Stewarts Lane and Hither Green engines were transferred to Norwood Junction and Feltham, the latter engines (31923 and 31924) appearing on Clapham-Waterloo ECS workings as well as local freights. Some replaced 'E4's on the Oxted line goods and in May 1961 31911-31913, 31916 and 31922 went to Eastleigh to

replace the Urie 'H16' 4-6-2Ts and 'Z' 0-8-0Ts on the heavy Fawley oil trains. This lasted successfully until diesels reached that branch in November 1962.

In September 1962, 31924 was sent to Exmouth Junction for trials on the St David's-Exeter Central bank, as the 'Z' 0-8-0Ts , although effective, needed replacement fireboxes. In December it was joined by 31911-31914, 31916 and 31917 for banking and local freight work to Yeovil Junction and Exmouth. In July 1963 the Western Region assumed responsibility for lines west of Salisbury, and 31913 and 31917 were returned to the Southern Region, whilst 31923 was condemned with faulty cylinders. 31916 was withdrawn from service in July 1963 and 31911 and 31915 in October, when the rest were reallocated to the Southern Region following the dieselisation of all services in the West Country, and the need for banking at Exeter evaporated.

Norwood Junction engines had a couple of turns in South London and a trip to Willesden, but when Norwood closed to steam in January 1964, 31912-31914 and 31924 were sent to Feltham. 31913 was withdrawn in March 1964, but the last three spent the summer working empty stock to and from Waterloo and a few local goods from the Clapham Junction area. The last two, 31912 and 31914, were withdrawn in August 1964. None are preserved, and my personal reminiscences are limited to seeing them on heavy freights particularly around Clapham Junction in my trainspotting days.

31922 with an engineering train being loaded with chalk from the cutting at Knockholt to take to the Kent Coast to repair some of the damage caused by the 1953 floods. (Ken Whiteman)

31911, bunker first, heads a freight from Hither Green down the Dartford Loop between New Eltham and Sidcup, 12 November 1960. (David Clark)

31917 near Wood Lane Crossing with an eastbound freight from Feltham, 29 August 1963. (MLS Collection)

31920 at Lingfield with a perishable special freight of banana traffic, 1 June 1963. (David Clark)

31924 at Exeter Central on empty stock, 13 August 1963. (MLS Collection)

31924 at Exeter Central having banked a train from Exeter St David's, 17 August 1963. (MLS Collection)

Chapter 7

THE 'Z' 0-8-0TS

Design & Construction

The companies that made up the Southern Railway, particularly the LB&SCR and the SE&CR, seemed to have had a problem in designing and building genuine shunting and local goods engines, relying for the bulk of the time on life-expired locomotives designed for other purposes. The LB&SCR realised this in the 1870s, when they suddenly alighted on the 'E1' tank (see next chapter) but had little since other than the ten 'E2's – all 0-6-0Ts. The South Eastern had the Stirling 'R1's of 1888, but most subsequent designs of both railways concentrated more on passenger or mixed traffic tank engines such as the 'H' and 'E4' classes. Even the former L&SWR had only the Adams 1894 'G6' 0-6-0Ts apart from the four Urie 'G16' 4-8-0s designed for hump shunting and trip working at Feltham. The Southern companies had less heavy freight than their neighbours north of the Thames, and the freight they had was predominantly merchandise in brake-fitted vans rather than coal or steel or other heavy bulk traffic.

However, loads increased and small 0-6-0Ts of Victorian vintage were often underpowered for the needs. The Urie 4-8-0s were specialist engines built for hump yard work, of which the Southern Railway had none apart from Feltham. Maunsell had inherited a 1922 plan to build more of this class, but such engines were unnecessarily wasteful, overpowered for general work and their superheaters were not needed – indeed were uneconomic when shunting engines spent so long standing. His immediate priorities were to build badly needed passenger engines for boat train and express passenger work, where the Southern was getting much flak from the public media, so it was not until the late 1920s that Maunsell turned his attention to a specialist locomotive for yard shunting.

He adapted the 3-cylinder design of the U1's, to be followed by a similar thought process for heavy short distance freight – his 'W' 2-6-4Ts as described in the last chapter. The product was a 3-cylinder 0-8-0 tank engine with much superior adhesion to the Victorian 0-6-0Ts, although the initial eight locomotives which finally appeared in 1929 were not multiplied as the long-term solution to the shunting and trip working need came in the 1930s in the form of the diesel 0-6-0 shunting locomotive.

The cylinder dimensions, as stated earlier, were similar to those of the 'U1' mogul, but the inside cylinder was connected with Walschaerts valve gear, operated by two eccentrics on the crank axle instead of using the conjugated valve gear. The wheels were 4ft 8in in diameter and despite being an 0-8-0, the wheelbase was only 17ft 6in which gave it flexibility round the often sharp curvature in shunting yards. A standard Brighton boiler was used and a large Ashford style cab giving easy manoeuvrability for the crew during shunting operations. The water capacity at 1,500 gallons was relatively low, enough for a shunting engine and the bunker could hold three tons allowing it to remain out of the depot for long periods as long as water columns were accessible. The engines were built at Brighton Works, but were numbered in the 'A' series as the design work had been carried out at Ashford. However, in 1931 they did not receive the extra 1,000 as other Eastern Section locomotives with the 'A' prefix, but filled the vacant space in the Western Section number series as 950-957 numbers were unallocated.

Very little subsequent change occurred – vents were fitted in the 1940s to the cab roofs, presumably to give better ventilation. All passed to British Railways and they were

A portrait of the first locomotive of the class, A950, on a postcard, 1929. (F. Moore/John Scott-Morgan Collection)

A951, brand new after completion at Brighton Works and just released for running in, in the plain SR goods black livery, 1929. (John Scott-Morgan Collection)

950 at Eastleigh in a line of locomotives awaiting repair, including a Urie 'S15' and 'H15', c1935. (John Scott-Morgan Collection)

956 and Billington 'B4X' 4-4-0 2054 at Bricklayers Arms shed, c1935. (John Scott-Morgan Collection)

951 at an unknown location, c1935. (John Scott-Morgan Collection)

952 and 'O2' 0-4-4T 204 at Eastleigh, c1938. (MLS Collection)

Two 'Z' 0-8-0Ts, 956 and an unidentified one, at Hither Green shed, 7 May 1939. (MLS Collection)

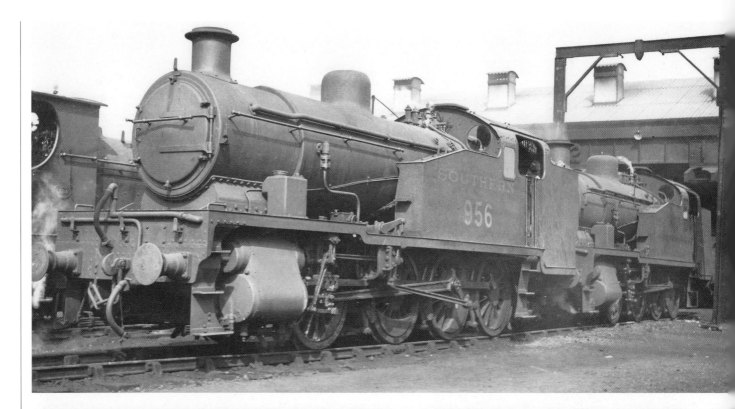

951 in the immediate post-war period, recently repainted in Southern wartime black with Bulleid style numerals and tankside lettering, at Eastleigh, c1947. (John Scott-Morgan Collection)

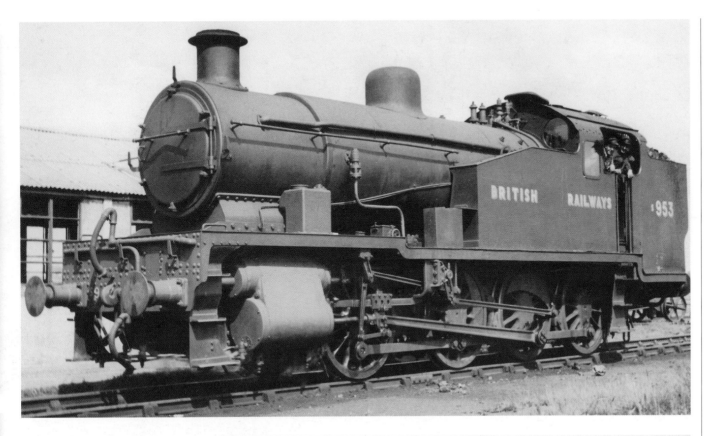

s953 immediately after nationalisation at Hither Green depot, 21 May 1948. (MLS Collection)

30951, a 'K' 2-6-0 and an Ivatt '2MT' 2-6-2T at Three Bridges, 15 July 1954. (MLS Collection)

30955 ex works at Eastleigh, 10 September 1959. (Colin Boocock)

The casting of a new cylinder block for a class 'Z' at Eastleigh Works, 14 April 1960. (Colin Boocock)

30952 with the latest BR lion & wheel icon, on Eastleigh shed, shortly before withdrawal, 16 June 1962.
(N. Fields/MLS Collection)

30950 at Exmouth Junction, 5 July 1962.
(R.C. Riley)

then renumbered 30950-30957. Their shunting duties were taken over by the BR 08 diesel shunters in the 1950s and, after a final spell as bankers, were found to require major firebox repairs and as some 'W' 2-6-4Ts were surplus by this time (see last chapter) all were withdrawn in 1962. None was preserved.

Operation

The eight 'Z's were built for heavy shunting and were allocated to the large London marshalling yards at Hither Green and Norwood Junction, and the Western Section yards at Eastleigh and Exmouth Junction. The 'G16' 4-8-0Ts continued to supply the hump shunting and trip working needs at Feltham. The plan to base one at Nine Elms was not followed through as curvature and clearances for the engine, which had a large overhang beyond the coupled wheels, were too tight. The order for a further ten similar locomotives was cancelled when freight traffic activity fell away in the early 1930s because of the Depression. The allocation was static until the Second World War when three were loaned to Scotland between December 1942 and May 1943 to cope with major military activity there.

In the 1950s, the shunting requirements at the Southern Region's main yards were met by the Southern diesel shunters, then the BR '08' development. In 1949 the allocation had been:

Hither Green:	30950, 30951, 30953, 30955
Eastleigh:	30952, 30956
Exmouth Junction:	30954
Salisbury:	30957

The Hither Green engines covered both Hither Green and Norwood Junction yards.

Then, in the 1950s, many changes took place as diesel shunters were allocated and changes occurred as lone engine allocations were affected by the need for Works attention. In the autumn of 1949, the four Hither Green engines were reallocated – 30950 moved to Eastleigh, 30951 to Gillingham, 30953 to Ashford and 30955 to Feltham, then Nine Elms. 30955 moved on further to Ashford in January 1952. Further changes took place in 1953:

30950 to Brighton
30951 to Three Bridges
30952 to Dover

30950 moved on to Tonbridge in 1954, 30952 returned to Ashford, 30955 to Brighton and at the end of the year 30953 went to Templecombe to assist with the reversal movements of traffic to and from the former Somerset & Dorset line.

In 1955, 30950 and 30951 joined 30952 at Ashford and 30956 joined 30957 at Salisbury for a few months before moving on to Exmouth Junction, where it replaced 30954 which went to Salisbury. Between 1955 and 1959 there was always one at Templecombe, Salisbury's 30954 swapping with 30953 when that engine was not available. 30956, after its short sojourn in Salisbury, went to Exmouth Junction. After all these exchanges the allocation settled down between 1956 and 1959 as follows:

Ashford:	30950, 30951, 30952

Brighton:	30955
Exmouth Junction:	30956
Salisbury:	30953, 30954, 30957

Salisbury normally supplied either 30953 or 30954 to Templecombe. 30957 seemed to be the only one of the eight engines that stayed in one location throughout the 1950s. Then in January 1959 seven of the eight 'Z's went to Exmouth Junction (excluding 30957 which still stayed for the time being at Salisbury, although it joined its sisters later) to take over the banking between Exeter St David's and Exeter Central from the E1/R 0-6-2Ts. Then, in the autumn of 1962, with the 'Z's requiring significant repairs to their fireboxes and with the pending transfer of the Exeter area to the Western Region, GWR pannier tanks replaced them, until redundant 'W' 2-6-4Ts from elsewhere on the Southern took over. The 'Z's were all withdrawn at the end of 1962.

There was an attempt to retain one of them, 30952, for restoration and use on the Bluebell Railway and it was stored at Exmouth Junction for a few months before spending 1963 and 1964 at Fratton in the company of other Southern engines laid aside for possible preservation. However, the attempt failed and it moved to Eastleigh in 1965 and then on to a South Wales scrap yard.

Personal Reminiscences

This was a class of engine that I saw virtually nothing of in my trainspotting days – the only one I saw was 30955 in 1951 or 1952 which I glimpsed from the window

30956, shortly after repair and repainting at Eastleigh, on a goods approaching Totton, 12 May 1951. (MLS Collection)

30956 on an Eastleigh-Fawley freight crossing Redbridge Causeway, c1952. (J. Davenport/ MLS Collection)

The 'Z' allocated to Salisbury and sub-shedded at Templecombe to assist reversing movements of S&D trains calling at Templecombe, 30953, is easing a Bath-Bournemouth train from Templecombe Upper down to the junction to resume its journey to Bournemouth, 1956. (MLS Collection)

30956 shunting empty ex LMS coaches at Exeter Central, 15 August 1961. (MLS Collection)

30952 shunting empty coaching stock at Exeter Central station, 5 July 1961. (R.C. Riley)

of a Hampton Court electric unit as I was passing the entrance to Nine Elms depot at Queen's Road. Then, later in June 1962, I had grabbed the opportunity to go right through to Plymouth with a 'King' – 6018 was on the 9.30am SO Paddington to Newquay. By the time we arrived in Plymouth, there was no certainty

of steam back via the Western route, so I took the 3-coach Plymouth portion of a Waterloo train behind unrebuilt 34030. We acquired extra coaches from Padstow and Bude en route, so we had sufficient tonnage to require a banker from St David's up to Exeter Central station. The previous time I had experienced a

banker there, it was an E1/R. This time, a burly 'Z' 0-8-0T buffered up to our rear coach – it was that very same 30955. 35010 was waiting for us for the run forward to Woking. By the time of my next Southern trip to the West Country in 1963 they too had gone and had been replaced by a couple of 'W's.

30957 at Exeter St David's banking a train headed by unrebuilt 'Battle of Britain' 34068 *Kenley* to Exeter Central, 23 June 1962. A rebuilt Bulleid light pacific waits behind to take over the next Southern service bound for Waterloo. (R.C. Riley)

Chapter 8

THE 'E1/R' 0-6-2TS

Design & Construction

In the 1870s the London Brighton and South Coast Railway used a variety of locomotives between duties and pensioned-off main line engines to engage in necessary shunting, but often the locomotives used were unsuitable and inefficient for this work. William Stroudley therefore designed and Brighton Works built an 0-6-0 tank engine specifically for short distance goods and shunting activities. The first six class 'E' locomotives, later designated 'E1', appeared between September 1874 and March 1875 and ultimately eighty were constructed, most in 1877 and 1878, the final six not appearing until 1891. They were numbered between 85 and 164 and, in the LB&SCR tradition, were all named after locations, many of them continental states, cities and towns in France, Germany and Italy.

Their coupled wheels were 4ft 6in in diameter, boiler pressure 140lb psi, heating surface 856sqft, with two inside cylinders of 17in x 24in. Water capacity was just 900 gallons and the bunker held 1¾ tons of coal. The engine weighed 39 tons 10cwt. A number were withdrawn from 1908, but the rest were retained following increased freight activity caused by the First

World War. Sixty-two were still extant at the Grouping in 1923, but in 1925, twenty-five were surplus to requirements and offered for sale. One of them, B110, formerly named *Burgundy*, was sold to Cannock & Rugeley Colliery Company in 1927 and survived there long enough to be rescued when its work there was over and was preserved in several locations including the East Somerset Railway, eventually to be restored in the identity of one of the four Isle of Wight 'E1's. The intention is to restore it as W2 *Yarmouth*.

More 'E1's were declared surplus in 1926/7, but Maunsell decided to rebuild ten of them for some of the more arduous branch line activities in the West Country. It was considered cheaper to undertake this rebuilding than to construct more new locomotives suitable for this work – presumably the 'O2's were not considered powerful enough and the Drummond 'M7's were required all over the former LSWR system. The locomotives chosen for rebuilding were Nos. 94, 95, 96, 124, 135, 608 (formerly 108, renumbered to the LB&SCR duplicate list in 1916), 610, 695, 696 and 697 (ex 99, 103, 104 and 105 respectively).

The main changes required for the rebuilding were the lengthening of

the frames at the rear to support an 'N' class pony truck and an enlarged bunker, larger tanks with an extra 348 gallon capacity and a new closed-in cab as found on some former SE&CR tank engines. The main dimension changes were:

Diameter of new
    trailing 'radial' wheels: 3ft 1in
Boiler pressure: 170lb psi
Heating surface: 924sqft
Grate area: 15½sqft
Water capacity: 1,260 gallons
Coal capacity: 2¼ tons
Tractive effort: 18,560lb

Despite these increases, the weight was kept to 39 tons 12cwt empty, but with the increased water and coal capacity weighed 50 tons 5cwt in full working order.

The first rebuilds (Nos. 94 and 95) were undertaken at Brighton Works in 1927, with 96, 124, 135, 608, 695 and 696 in 1928 and the final pair, 610 and 697, in January 1929. They were painted passenger green as their purpose was branch passenger work rather than goods or shunting. Initially they were classified as class 'E7', but this was changed to 'E1/R' (the 'R' standing for 'Radial' rather than 'Rebuild').

Although they performed well enough, they could be rough-riding on the branch tracks and

LBSCR 'E' tank, No.99 *Bordeaux*, built in 1874, renumbered 610 in June 1922, and rebuilt as an 'E1/R' 0-6-2T in January 1929, which worked in North Devon, renumbered 2610 and 32610 until withdrawn in March 1956, c1900. (MLS Collection)

An 'E' tank, 2138, at about the time when sister engine 2135 was rebuilt as an 'E1/R', seen here at Exeter, c1932. (MLS Collection)

E1/R 2096 as rebuilt in October 1928 and renumbered and painted in SR lined green livery, at Eastleigh, c1932. (John Scott-Morgan Collection)

2608 at Exmouth Junction shed, Urie 'H15' 484 in the background, 28 March 1932. (F. Moore/ MLS Collection)

2697, whilst allocated to Exmouth Junction for banking and shunting work, still in plain black Southern Railway wartime livery and as yet still bearing its SR number although two and a half years after nationalisation, 22 August 1950.
(John Scott-Morgan Collection)

this caused some complaints, especially from passengers as the roughness transferred itself to the single passenger vehicle adjacent to the engine which was the normal consist of most of those local country services. Five were therefore rebalanced (now renumbered 2094, 2095, 2096, 2608 and 2610) and restored to the passenger services whilst the other three were restricted to shunting, local freight or banking duties.

The Bulleid unlined dark green with new style lettering and

numerals was applied to 2124 in 1939, followed by 2608 and 2695 in 1940. 2095 and 2610 in 1940 and 2095 in 1941 were painted unlined light green with the Bulleid style lettering and numerals. After that any repainting was in standard wartime plain black, starting with 2135 in 1941. On nationalisation in 1948 they, with all SR locomotives, had 30,000 added to their numbers and initially several were repainted in the BR lined black mixed traffic livery.

The first 'E1/R' (32094) was withdrawn in 1955, and the

last survivor was 32697 which remained on banking duties at Exeter until the end of the 1959 summer timetable. Its final mileage was 1,541,086, a very high mileage for a shunting and branch line engine, although its life as 105 *Morlaix* lasted from September 1876 until retired as 32697 in December 1959, an active lifespan of eighty-three years. A couple of others (32095 and 32124) achieved nearly 1.5 million miles. The lowest was 32135 at 1.12 million.

32124 ex works in BR plain black, Eastleigh Works, 1948. (Ken Wightman)

32135 waiting for the next train to bank to Central at Exeter St David's, c1952. (MLS Collection)

32135 at Exmouth Junction, 5 May 1957. (R.C. Riley)

Operation

After rebuilding at Brighton Works and dealing with a few teething problems, the first two, B94 and B95, were sent to the West Country. The rest followed although three (B610, 696 and 697) worked local goods and shunting turns out of Fratton in the winter of 1928/9. Exmouth Junction retained two (B94 and 696) for shunting and carriage pilot work, the remainder going to Barnstaple. Their duties included in particular the branches to Torrington and Halwill Junction.

After the rebalancing to eradicate public complaints of rough riding, the following five were allocated to the Barnstaple sub-shed: 2094-2096, 2608, 2610. The other unmodified engines acted as station pilots, shunted Fremington Quay or worked shunting and local freight turns from Exmouth Junction. In 1938 four of these – 2124, 2135, 2695 and 2697 – replaced the 'G6' 0-6-0Ts as bankers from Exeter St David's up the 1 in 37 to Exeter Central.

During the war, 2608 and 2610 spent several months at Plymouth shunting, but most resumed their pre-war work afterwards and the four bankers remained active at Exeter, interrupted only by Works visits for repair – Eastleigh initially and then Brighton after mid-1954.

32094 was transferred to Plymouth in 1949 for shunting in Plymouth Friary Goods Yard. In 1953 Ivatt 2MT 2-6-2Ts appeared at Barnstaple and took over the branch working to Halwill Junction and Torrington, two 'E1/Rs' (32095 and 32096) joining 32094 at Plymouth Friary, the others going to Exmouth Junction to share the banking and shunting duties.

After withdrawal began, banking duties from Exeter St David's were shared with 'M7's until the demise of 32124 in February, 32135 in April and 32697 in August 1959, when the 'Z' 0-8-0Ts took over. This last survivor wandered across the

2096 being prepared on shed at Barnstaple before the day's work, c1932. (John Scott-Morgan Collection)

2095 in SR green livery at Halwill Junction, c1934. (K. Nunn/John Scott-Morgan Collection)

2124 with the one coach branch train crossing Torrington Viaduct, c1934. (Lens of Sutton/John Scott-Morgan Collection)

2695 at Torrington with the branch train for Halwill Junction, c1935. (John Scott-Morgan Collection)

2697 shunting at Exmouth Junction, 22 August 1950. (John Scott-Morgan Collection)

system in the Autumn of 1959 once displaced from Exeter and was noted at Salisbury, Eastleigh and Eastbourne before reaching Ashford for scrapping in December.

Personal Reminiscences

In the summer of 1952 (16 August) I travelled with my parents and two younger sisters to Paignton for our annual seaside holiday. We had come down from Surbiton on the 7.38am Waterloo-West Country behind Nine Elms' 30787 and Salisbury's 35007 and, to my boyish surprise and delight, found that our three-quarters of a mile descent from Exeter Central to St David's was to be triple-headed! Watching the three

2695 banking the observation coach at the rear of the *Devon Belle* Pullman train, about to enter the short tunnel near the summit of the 1 in 37 before Exeter Central station, c1950. (MLS Collection)

2608 at Halwill Junction being oiled by the driver before returning to Torrington with the branch train, 8 August 1948. (John Scott-Morgan Collection)

'E1/R' 32124 pilots an 'M7' 0-4-4T on a freight at the Exeter Central summit of the 1 in 36 from St David's, c1951. (MLS Collection)

engines blowing off steam furiously as they backed under the overbridge at the west end of the station, I rejoiced in three 'cops' – Exmouth Junction's 34025 *Whimple,* my 'first' 'T9', 30702, with the Padstow portion and an engine shape then totally unknown to me, which was the St David's 'E1/R' banker, black 32135, returning down the hill to base, coupled to us to reduce the occupation of that busy stretch of line on an August Saturday – especially crucial at the junction with the WR main line at the foot of the bank.

When the fortnight was over and my Ian Allan WR ABC had

32696 in BR mixed traffic lined black livery at Halwill Junction with the Torrington branch train just before replacement by Ivatt '2MT' 2-6-2Ts, c1952. (John Scott-Morgan Collection)

32135 pilots an unrebuilt 'West Country' pacific out of Exeter St David's with a freight bound for Exmouth Junction yard, c1956. (Norman Harrop/ MLS Collection)

32695 and 32135 stand ready in the banker siding at Exeter St David's awaiting the next Southern train for assisting to Exeter Central, 20 July 1956. (R.C. Riley)

The pair of 'E1/Rs' that I had most often, 32124 and 32135, awaiting their next turn of duty to bank trains to Exeter Central, standing here at Exeter St David's adjacent to Red Cow Crossing, 2 August 1956. (MLS Collection)

been much filled, our return from St David's behind a single light pacific (34058) was banked by 32124, better presented in BR mixed traffic lined black. Two further West Country holidays in 1953 and 1956 to Paignton again and Ilfracombe were once more banked on the return journeys by 32697 and 32135 respectively. In 1954 during a family holiday in Sidmouth, I spent a day trainspotting at Exeter St David's and travelled up the bank twice to Central just to enjoy the slog up the gradient, the Bulleid pacific at the front slithering and sliding into the tunnel near the top of the bank while the valiant 'E1/R's exhaust reverberated round the cutting and the tunnel walls at the back. I travelled both times in the rear coach just for the fun of it, getting both 0-6-2Ts on banking duty that day, 32135 and 32697.

I never did get a run behind an 'E1/R' on one of the North Devon branches. When I eventually visited the Halwill Junction-Torrington branch and travelled through the purple rhododendron-filled woods, it was behind an Ivatt 'Mickey Mouse' tank, 41314.

Chapter 9

THE SUCCESSORS

As with most of my previous Pen & Sword books, I have given some thought to the successors of the classes in the *Locomotive Portfolios*, whether a natural design development or locomotives designed for the same end purpose in location. Oliver Bulleid's clear intention for the type of work carried out by the moguls and tank engines was his ambitious and controversial 'Leader' class, but since it never came to fruition beyond an initial construction and unsuccessful tests, these intended locomotives cannot be considered as successors.

The first true successors to appear were the LMS Fairburn 2-6-4Ts which were a concept that the Southern Railway had struggled to develop with the 'Rivers' and took up many of the duties in Kent and Sussex that the SR moguls had previously dominated. Later, the BR Standard '4' 2-6-4Ts were a development of the LMS design and continued the same role, extending it in the later steam era to the South Western Section around Eastleigh and Bournemouth. As they had a wider route availability than the LMS Fairburn tanks, the SR allocation was significantly augmented in 1959 in exchange

for the Fairburn tanks which were repatriated to the LMR and NER.

The BR Standard '4' 2-6-0 was an obvious successor to the SR moguls, with smaller coupled wheels than the 'N's, but an ability to cover work performed by the 'U's as well as the 'N's. Indeed, the first batch allocated to Eastleigh, and even more obviously the ten (76053-62) allocated to Redhill immediately took over diagrams directly previously worked by 'U's and 'N's. Later, in the last couple of years of Southern Region steam, they took over many of the Maunsell mogul diagrams in the Bournemouth-Weymouth area.

Fairburn LMS
2-6-4T 42099, built at Brighton, 1951, seen here immediately after construction, 1951.
(MLS Collection)

The old and new order – newly built 42100 stands in front of ex LB&SCR pacific tank engine 32326, at Tunbridge Wells West shed, 7 October 1950. (MLS Collection)

42097 at London Bridge with a train for Oxted and Tunbridge Wells West, 21 July 1951. (MLS Collection)

80082, a transfer from the LMR at Bletchley, exchanged for LMS Fairburn tanks, at Eastleigh in the company of Urie 'S15', 30507, 8 June 1963. (MLS Collection)

80033, allocated to the Southern Region from the beginning, entering Tunbridge Wells with a Tonbridge-Brighton train, 23 May 1959. (MLS Collection)

76005, shortly after construction and allocated to Eastleigh, at Bournemouth depot, 1953. (Real Photographs/ MLS Collection)

76053, the prototype Redhill Standard '4' with BR1B tender at the end of its life entering Swanage station with the branch train from Wareham, 20 June 1966. (MLS Collection)

APPENDIX

'N' 2-6-0

Dimensions

Cylinders (2)	19in x 28in
Coupled wheels	5ft 6in
Pony truck wheels	3ft 1in
Heating surface	1,728.5sqft
Grate area	25sqft
Boiler pressure	200lb psi
Axleload	17½ tons
Weight	
Engine	59 tons 8cwt
Tender	39 tons 5cwt
Total	98 tons 13cwt
Tender capacity	
Water	3,500 gallons
Coal	5 tons

Weight Diagram

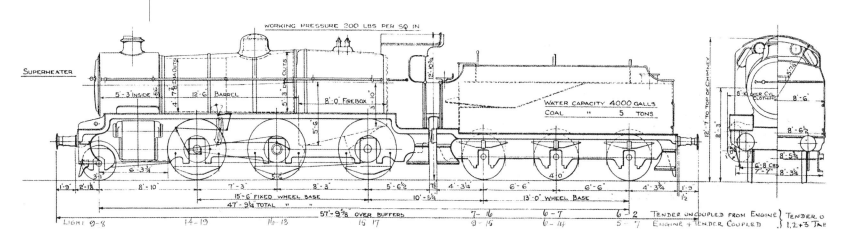

Statistics

Loco No.	Built	Frame renewal	Withdrawn	Mileage	Comments
810	8/17		3/64	1,066,244	All renumbered A810
811	6/20		9/65		etc in 1/23 and 1810
812	8/20		6/64		etc in 7/31 & 31810 etc
813	9/20		10/63		in 1/48
814	11/20		7/64		
815	12/20		5/63	1,012,590	
816	12/21*		1/66		
817	1/22		1/64		
818	3/22		9/63		
819	5/22**		1/64		
820	8/22		8/63		
821	10/22		5/64		
823	5/23		11/62		
824	8/23		9/63		
A825	12/23		10/63		A825 – A875 built at
A826	6/24		9/63	996,447	Woolwich Arsenal or
A827	5/24		9/63		from parts assembled
A828	6/24		9/63		at Ashford
A829	7/24	10/60 (full)	1/64		
A830	6/24	11/55 (part)	1/64		
A831	6/24	8/60 (part)	4/65		
A832	7/24		1/64		
A833	7/24	6/59 (full)	2/64		
A834	7/24		9/64		
A835	7/24	5/57 (full)	9/64		
A836	7/24		12/63		
A837	7/24	2/61 (full)	9/64		
A838	7/24	6/57 (part)	2/64		
A839	8/24		12/63		
A840	8/24	2/57 (part)	9/64		
A841	8/24		3/64		
A842	8/24	12/57 (part)	9/65		
A843	8/24	8/58 (part)	9/64		
A844	9/24		12/63		
A845	9/24	3/60 (full)	9/64		
A846	1/25	5/59 (part)	9/64		
A847	2/25		10/63		
A848	2/25	10/55 (full)	2/64		
A849	2/25		6/64		
A850	2/25***		1/64		
A851	2/25		9/63		
A852	3/25		9/63		
A853	4/25	7/60 (part)	9/64		
A854	3/25	8/57 (part)	6/64		

*Steam conservation experiment 1930-2
** Worthington Feed Water Pump, 1924
***Marshall valve gear 1933-4

Loco No.	Built	Frame renewal	Withdrawn	Mileage	Comments
A855	3/25	12/55 (full)	9/64		
A856	3/25		9/64		
A857	4/25		1/64		
A858	5/25	5/61 (full)	12/65		
A859	4/25		9/64		
A860	4/25		11/63		
A861	6/25		5/63		
A862	5/25	4/60 (part)	4/65		
A863	5/25	2/61 (full)	7/63		
A864	6/25	1/59 (part)	1/64	1,033, 839	
A865	6/25		9/63		
A866	11/25		1/66		
A867	6/25		7/63		
A868	7/25	12/60 (part)	1/64		
A869	7/25	2/58 (part)	8/64		
A870	7/25		4/64	1,110,161	
A871	7/25	3/61 (full)	12/63		
A872	8/25		5/63		
A873	9/25		1/66		
A874	9/25	5/57 (part)	3/64		
A875	8/25		8/64		
1400	7/32	1/58 (part)	6/64	860,934	from 1400 renumbered 31400 etc, 1/48
1401	8/32		7/65		
1402	8/32		8/63		
1403	8/32		6/63	792,850	
1404	10/32		12/63	769, 597	
1405	11/32	3/57 (part)	6/66		
1406	1/32	1/60 (full)	9/64		
1407	8/32		7/63		
1408	9/32	4/57 (part)	6/66		
1409	10/32		11/62		
1410	11/33		11/64		
1411	11/33		4/66		
1412	12/33		8/64		
1413	1/34	5/60 (full)	6/64		
1414	1/34		11/62		

'N1' 3-cyl. 2-6-0
Dimensions

Cylinders (3)	16in x 28in
Coupled wheel diameter	5ft 6in
Pony Truck	3ft 1in
Heating surface	1,728.5sqft
Grate area	25sqft
Boiler pressure	190lb psi
Axleload	18 tons 5cwt

Weight
Engine   62 tons 15cwt
Tender   39 tons 5cwt
Total   102 tons 0cwt
Tender capacity
Water   3,500 gallons
Coal   5 tons

Statistics

Loco.No.	Built	First depot	SR No.	BR No.	Last depot	Withdrawn	Mileage
822	3/23	Bricklayers Arms	1822	31822	Stewarts Lane	11/62	859,851
A876	3/30	New Cross Gate	1876	31876	Stewarts Lane	11/62	731,447
A877	4/30	New Cross Gate	1877	31877	Stewarts Lane	11/62	762,536
A878	4/30	New Cross Gate	1878	31878	Stewarts Lane	11/62	784,137
A879	4/30	New Cross Gate	1879	31879	Stewarts Lane	11/62	714,823
A880	11/30	New Cross Gate	1880	31880	Stewarts Lane	11/62	762,425

Weight Diagram

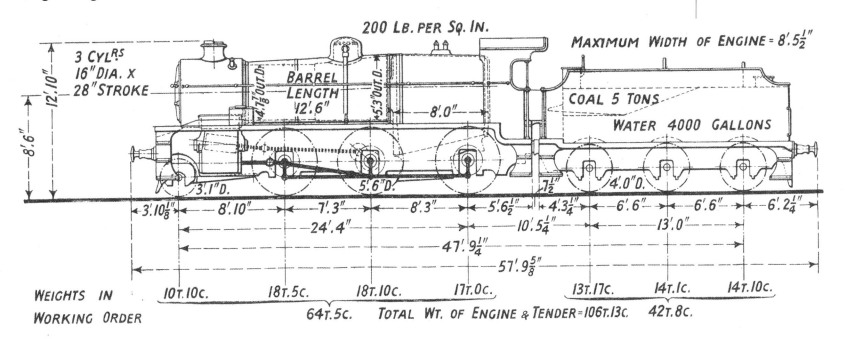

'K' ('River') 2-6-4T

Dimensions

Cylinders (2)	19in x 28in
Coupled wheel diameter	6ft 0in
Pony truck & trailing wheels	3ft 1in
Boiler pressure	200lb psi
Total heating surface	1,850sqft
Grate area	25sqft
Axleload	18 tons 10cwt
Weight	82 tons 12cwt
Tractive effort (85%)	23,870 lbs
Water capacity	2,000 gallons
Coal capacity	2½ tons

Weight Diagram

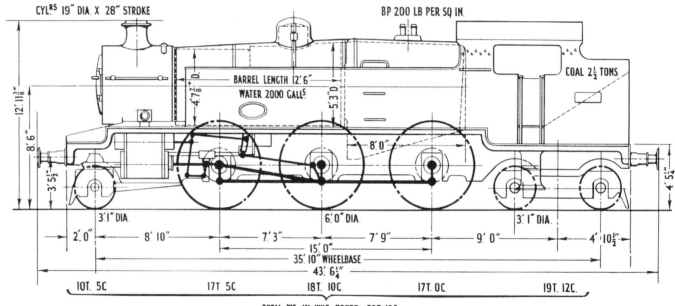

Statistics

SR No.		Built	Rebuilt as 'U'	Mileage as 'K' River
A790	*River Avon*	6/17	6/28	313,973
A791	*River Adur*	5/25	7/28	63,730
A792	*River Arun*	5/25	7/28	69,994
A793	*River Ouse*	5/25	6/28	64,040
A794	*River Rother*	5/25	6/28	63,185
A795	*River Medway*	6/25	6/28	52,478
A796	*River Stour*	6/25	7/28	52,405

A797	*River Mole*	6/25	7/28	49,534
A798	*River Wey*	6/25	8/28	47.975
A799	*River Test*	6/25	7/28	60,932
A800	*River Cray*	7/26	12/28	40,128
A801	*River Darenth*	7/26	7/28	42,292
A802	*River Cuckmere*	8/26	7/28	43,252
A803	*River Itchen*	8/26	6/28	36,599
A804	*River Tamar*	9/26	6/28	37,218
A805	*River Camel*	10/26	3/28	27,661
A806	*River Torridge*	10/26	6/28	22,027
A807	*River Axe*	11/26	6/28	25,376
A808	*River Char*	11/26	7/28	17,348
A809	*River Dart*	12/26	7/28	16,061

'K1' (3–cylinder 'River') 2-6-4T

Dimensions

As for 'K' (River) except:

Cylinders (3)	16in x 28in
Axleload	19 tons 5cwt
Weight	88 tons 15cwt
Tractive effort (85%)	25,390 lb

Statistics

SR No.		Built	Rebuilt as U1	SR No. (1931)	BR No.	Withdrawn	Mileage
A890	*River Frome*	12/25	6/28	1890	31890	6/63	1,026,340

Weight Diagram (Ashford Drawing)

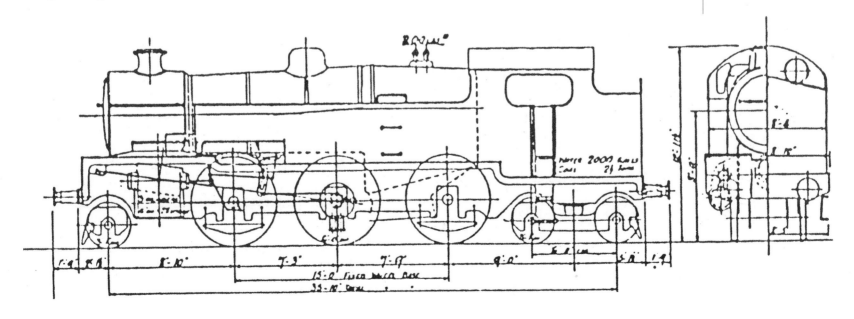

'U' 2-6-0

Dimensions

Cylinders (2)	19in x 26in
Coupled wheel diameter	6ft 0in
Pony Truck wheels	3ft 1in
Boiler pressure	200lb psi
Heating surface	1,728½sqft
Grate area	25sqft
Axleload	18 tons 16cwt (18 tons 5cwt - 16xx series)
Weight:	
Engine	63 tons 0cwt (62 tons 6cwt – 16xx series)
Tender	40 tons 10cwt
Total	103 tons 10cwt (102 tons 16cwt – 16xx series)
Tractive effort	23,866lb
Water capacity	3,500 or 4,000 gallons
Coal capacity	5 tons

Weight Diagram (as built, and below, as oil-burner)

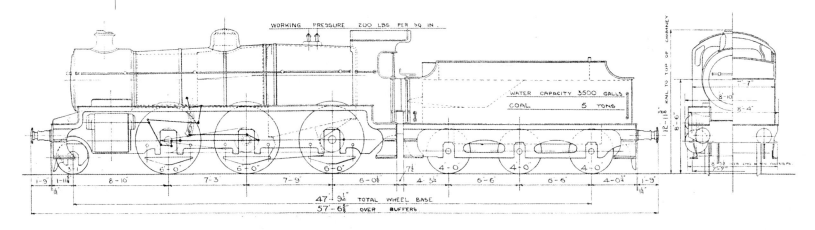

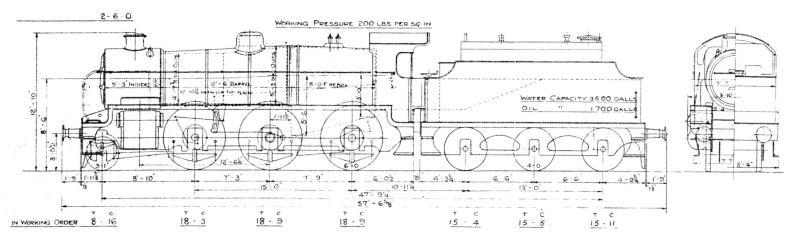

Statistics

SR No.	Built	Rebuilt	BR No.	Frame 11/60	allocation rebuilt	Withdrawn	Mileage
790 (A790)	7/17	6/28	31790	-	Guildford	5/65	
A791	5/25	7/28	31791	3/60	Eastleigh	6/66	
A792	5/25	7/28	31792	9/58	Yeovil	9/64	
A793	5/25	6/28	31793	-	Eastleigh	5/64	
A794	5/25	6/28	31794	-	Eastleigh	6/63	1,155,902
A795	6/25	6/28	31795	2/58	Eastleigh	6/63	1,115, 651
A796	6/25	7/28	31796	1/61	Eastleigh	1/64	
A797	6/25	7/28	31797	-	Guildford	1/64	
A798	6/25	8/28	31798	-	Yeovil	9/64	
A799	6/25	7/28	31799	-	Redhill	2/65	
A800	7/26	12/28	31800	-	Guildford	10/65	
A801	7/26	7/28	31801	-	Eastleigh	6/64	
A802	8/26	7/28	31802	1/59	Yeovil	9/64	
A803	8/26	6/28	31803	-	Eastleigh	3/66	
A804	9/26	6/28	31804	-	Eastleigh	6/64	
A805	10/26	3/28	31805	-	Yeovil	8/63	
A806	10/26	6/28	31806	11/57	Basingstoke	1/64	1,099,647 Preserved
A807	11/26	6/28	31807	-	Redhill	1/64	
A808	11/26	7/28	31808	-	Eastleigh	1/66	1,052,330
A809	12/26	7/28	31809	9/60	Eastleigh	1/66	
A610	8/28		31610	-	Guildford	12/62	1,222,907
A611	8/28		31611	-	Basingstoke	10/63	
A612	7/28		31612	-	Guildford	5/63	
A613	6/28		31613	3/58	Eastleigh	1/64	1,092,674
A614	7/28		31614	2/57	Yeovil	11/63	
A615	8/28		31615	6/60	Guildford	10/63	
A616	9/28		31616	-	Redhill	6/64	
A617	10/28		31617	2/61	Nine Elms	1/64	
A618	10/28		31618	-	Eastleigh	1/64	1,143,942 Preserved
A619	12/28		31619	11/60	Eastleigh	12/65	
A620	11/28		31620	-	Eastleigh	4/65	
A621	12/28		31621	2/55	Nine Elms	10/64	
A622	1/29		31622	11/60	Guildford	1/64	
A623	1/29		31623	3/56	Guildford	12/63	
A624	2/29		31624	5/56	Nine Elms	6/64	
A625	3/39		31625	1/59	Guildford	1/64	Preserved
A626	3/29		31626	-	Eastleigh	1/64	
A627	4/29		31627	-	Guildford	10/65	
A628	4/29		31628	1/57	Guildford	6/64	
A629	12/29*		31629	-	Eastleigh	1/64	
A630	2/31		31630	-	Guildford	11/62	987,941
A631	3/31		31631	?	Guildford	9/63	
A632	3/31		31632	-	Yeovil	9/64	
A633	3/31		31633	9/60	Guildford	12/63	
A634	4/31		31634	4/55	Nine Elms	12/63	

* pulverised fuel 1929-1932

SR No.	Built	Rebuilt	BR No.	Frame 11/60 allocation rebuilt		Withdrawn	Mileage
A635	4/31		31635	1/59	Guildford	12/63	
A636	4/31		31636	-	Guildford	6/63	
A637	5/31		31637	10/59	Yeovil	9/63	
A638	5/31		31638	-	Guildford	1/64	Preserved
A639	5/31		31639	-	Eastleigh	6/66	

'U1' 3-cyl .2-6-0

Dimensions

Cylinders (3)	16in x 28in
Coupled wheels	6ft 0in
Pony truck	3ft 1in
Boiler pressure	200lb psi
Heating surface	1,728½sqft
Grate area	25sqft
Axleload	18 tons 10cwt
Weight – engine	65 tons 6cwt
– tender	42 tons 8cwt
– total	107 tons 14cwt
Water capacity	4,000 gallons
Coal capacity	5 tons
Tractive effort	25,387lb

Weight Diagram

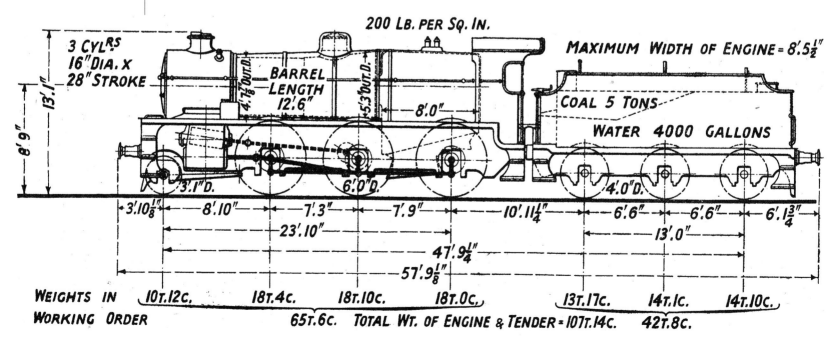

Statistics

SR No.	Built	SR No. (1931)	BR No.	Withdrawn	Mileage
A890	6/28	1890	31890	6/63	1,026,340 (Rebuilt from 'K1')
A891	1/31	1891	31891	4/63	
A892	1/31	1892	31892	11/62	
A893	2/31	1893	31893	12/62	
A894	2/31	1894	31894	12/62	
A895	3/31	1895	31895	12/62	934,916
A896	3/31	1896	31896	12/62	
A897	3/31	1897	31897	11/62	938,012
A898	4/31	1898	31898	12/62	
A899	4/31	1899	31899	12/62	
A900	5/31	1900	31900	12/62	
1901	6/31	as built	31901	9/63	
1902	7/31		31902	11/62	
1903	7/31		31903	12/62	
1904	7/31		31904	11/62	
1905	8/31		31905	12/62	843,683
1906	9/31		31906	12/62	
1907	9/31		31907	12/62	
1908	10/31		31908	12/62	
1909	10/31		31909	12/62	
1910	11/31		31910	7/63	792,540

'W' 2-6-4T

Dimensions

Cylinders (3)	16 ½ in x 28in
Coupled wheel diameter	5ft 6in
Leading wheel diameter	3ft 1in
Trailing bogie wheels	3ft 1in
Boiler pressure	200lb psi
Total heating surface	1,810.6sqft
Grate area	25sqft
Weight	90 tons 14cwt
Axleload	19 tons 5cwt
Tractive effort (85%)	29,450lb
Water capacity	2000 gallons
Coal capacity	3½ tons

Weight Diagram

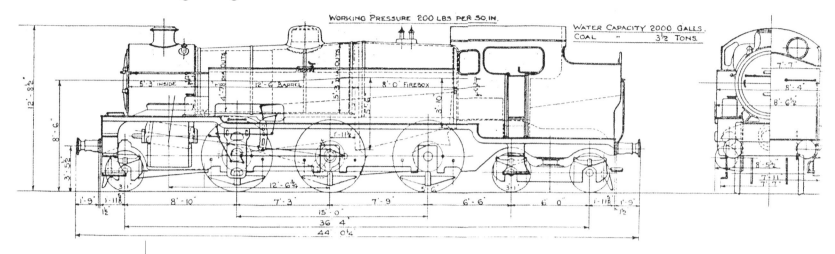

Statistics

SR No.	Built	BR No.	Withdrawn	Mileage
1911	1/32	31911	10/63	480,842
1912	1/32	31912	8/64	493,611
1913	1/32	31913	3/64	
1914	1/32	31914	8/64	
1915	2/32	31915	10/63	
1916	4/35	31916	7/63	
1917	4/35	31917	1/64	
1918	6/35	31918	8/63	
1919	7/35	31919	11/63	
1920	8/35	31920	7/63	
1921	10/35	31921	6/63	
1922	11/35	31922	8/63	
1923	1/36	31923	2/63	
1924	2/36	31924	7/64	424,096
1925	4/36	31925	11/63	

'Z' 0-8-0T

Dimensions

Cylinders (3)	16in x 28in
Coupled wheel diameter	4ft 8in
Boiler pressure	180lb psi
Total heating surface	1,279sqft
Grate area	18.6sqft
Weight	71 tons 12cwt
Tractive effort (85%)	29,380lb
Water capacity	1,500 gallons
Coal capacity	3 tons

Weight Diagram

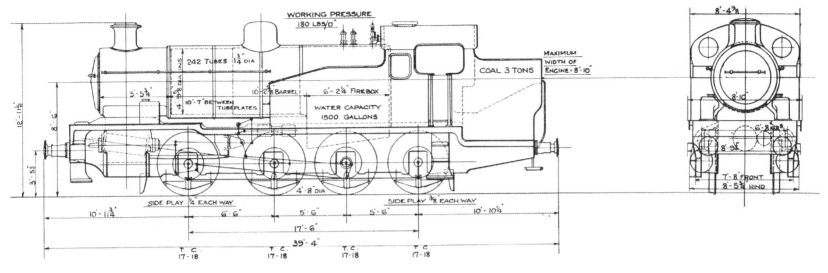

WORKING PRESSURE
180 LBS/☐"

242 TUBES 1¾ DIA

MAXIMUM
WIDTH OF
ENGINE = 8'-10"

COAL 3 TONS

5-5¾

10'-2⅝ BARREL

10'-7" BETWEEN
TUBEPLATES

6'-2¼ FIREBOX

WATER CAPACITY
1500 GALLONS

8'-4⅞

8'-10

6'-8⅝

8'-9½

7'-8 FRONT
8'-5¾ HIND

12'-1½

3'-5½

SIDE PLAY ¼ EACH WAY

SIDE PLAY ⅜ EACH WAY

4'-8 DIA

10'-1¾

6'-6

5'-6

5'-6

10'-10¼

17'-6"

39'-4"

T.C. 17-18   T.C. 17-18   T.C. 17-18   T.C. 17-18

TOTAL WEIGHT OF ENGINE IN WORKING ORDER   71 TONS. 12 CWTS.

WEIGHT OF ENGINE. EMPTY   56 TONS. 15 CWTS.

Statistics

SR No.	Built	First Depot	1931 SR No.	BR No.	Last depot	Withdrawn
A950	1929	Hither Green	950	30950	Exmouth Jcn	1962
A951	1929	Hither Green	951	30951	Exmouth Jcn	1962
A952	1929	Eastleigh	952	30952	Exmouth Jcn	1962
A953	1929	Hither Green	953	30953	Exmouth Jcn	1962
A954	1929	Exmouth Jcn	954	30954	Exmouth Jcn	1962
A955	1929	Hither Green	955	30955	Exmouth Jcn	1962
A956	1929	Eastleigh	956	30956	Exmouth Jcn	1962
A957	1929	Salisbury	957	30957	Exmouth Jcn	1962

'E1/R' 0-6-2T

Dimensions

Cylinders (2)	17in x 24in
Coupled wheel diameter	4ft 6in
Trailing wheel diameter	3ft 1in
Boiler pressure	170lb psi
Heating surface	924sqft
Grate area	15½sqft
Weight (empty)	39 tons 12cwt
Weight (working order)	50 tons 5cwt
Water capacity	1,260 gallons
Coal capacity	2¼ tons
Tractive effort	18,560lb

Weight Diagram

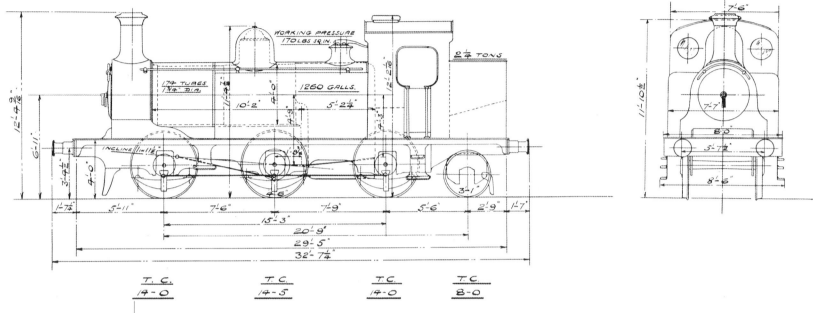

Statistics

LB&SCR No.	Name	Built (E1)	Renumbered	Rebuilt E1/R	SR no.	BR No.	Withdrawn	Mileage
94	*Shorwell*	11/1883		31/5/1927	2094	32094	4/55	
95	*Luccombe*	11/1883		27/5/1927	2095	32095	11/56	1,497,037
96	*Salzberg*	12/1883		18/10/1928	2096	32096	11/56	
99	*Bordeaux*	12/1874	610 6/22	14/1/1928	2610	32610	3/56	
103	*Normandy*	9/1876	695 6/13	27/10/1928	2695	32695	2/57	
104	*Brittany*	10/1876	696 10/13	20/12/1928	2696	32696	1/56	
105	*Morlaix*	9/1876	697 4/15	17/1/1929	2697	32697	12/59	1,541,086
108	*Jersey*	11/1876	608 1/16	13/11/1928	2608	32608	5/57	
124	*Bayonne*	8/1878		3/12/1928	2124	32124	2/59	1,482,336
135	*Foligno*	1/1879		26/11/1928	2135	32135	4/59	1,129,221

BIBLIOGRAPHY

BECKETT, **W.S.**, *The Xpress Locomotive Register, Vol 1, Southern Region: 1949-1961*, Xpress Publishing, 1998

BRADLEY, **D.L.**, *The Locomotive History of the South Eastern & Chatham Railway*, RCTS, 1980

BRADLEY, **D.L.**, *The Locomotives of the London Brighton & South Coast Railway, Part 1*, RCTS, 1969

COX, **E.S.**, *British Railways Standard Steam Locomotives*, Ian Allan, 1966

DONALDSON, **Drew**, **MCDONNELL, Bill**, **& O'NEILL, Jack**, *A Decade of Steam on CIE in the 1950s*, Railway Preservation Society of Ireland, 1974

ESSERY, Bob & JENKINSON, David, *An Illustrated History of LMS Locomotives, Vol 5, Post-Grouping Standard Designs*, Silver Link Publishing, 1989

FRYER, C.E.J., *The Rolling Rivers*, Platform 5, 1992

GOUDIE, Frank, *Metropolitan Steam Locomotives*, Capital Transport Publishing, 1990

NOCK, O.S., *Irish Steam*, David & Charles, 1982

PRITCHARD, Robert & HALL, Peter, *Preserved Locomotives of British Railways*, Platform 5, 2016

RCTS, *British Railways Standard Steam Locomotives, Volume 2: The 4-6-0 and 2-6-0 Classes*, RCTS, 2003

RCTS, *British Railways Standard Steam Locomotives, Volume 3: The Tank Engine Classes*, RCTS, 1997

RUSSELL, J.H., *A Pictorial Record of Southern Locomotives*, BCA/Haynes Publishing Group, 1991

SCOTT-MORGAN, John, *Maunsell Locomotives*, Ian Allan, 2002

SHEPHERD, Ernie, *Bulleid and the Turf Burner*, KRB Publications, 2004

INDEX

Photo Index